DIALOGUE
The YES Interviews

This edition 2019
Copyright © Jon Kirkman 2019
The moral right of the author has been asserted

A catalogue record for this book
is available from the British Library

ISBN: 978- 1-78972-377-9

Published by Classic Rock Vaults Books

rockahead@hotmail.com
www.classicrockvaults.com

Artwork & Cover Design: Alan Fennah
Transcription & Editing: Holly Quibell

Dialogue
The YES Interviews

JON KIRKMAN

Dedicated with much love and respect to:

Peter William Brockbanks
AKA Peter Banks

Christopher Russell Edward Squire
AKA Chris Squire

Contents

Foreword

The Word Is Dialogue
Jon Kirkman Knows Yes

He knows the band's music like few others; in fact, if there was an *Encyclopaedia Yes*, Jon would be the author.

Actually, there is an *Encyclopaedia Yes*. It's the book (or make that books) you are now holding in your hands (and let's admit it, *Dialogue* is a far more enticing title than *Encyclopaedia Yes*).

A well-known rock journalist and broadcaster for more than 40 true summers, Jon has spent countless hours with the many master musicians who have passed through the ranks of Yes of its five decades and counting career. During that time, he's established real relationships with the band, which is what makes *Dialogue* such an important and essential addition to the life of all of us Yes fans.

Throughout the interviews Jon has compiled for this series of books, you can read the ease and comfort that members like Geoff Downes and Alan White have with the author. Even erstwhile Yes singer Benoit David opens up significantly to Jon about his time in the band.

Especially poignant are the authors conversation with Chris Squire; Jon helped put together the first reissue of Squire's classic solo album, *Fish Out Of Water*, and their relationship is on display throughout *Dialogue*. I won't run down every moment worth reading here, though. That's for you to discover for yourself.

It's worth noting that this isn't the first time Jon has published this cornucopia of Yes goodness. There have been previous editions of *Dialogue*; the first was an expensive coffee table book released under the title *Time And A Word: The Yes Interviews* (2013). The second was a softcover titled also titled *Dialogue* (2017), which is now out of print, and didn't come cheap either. The exciting thing about the version you now have here is that it is both affordable and updated with even more content. You're also supporting the author directly with your purchase, and as someone who freelances at times, your patronage is always appreciated.

On a personal note, I've known Jon Kirkman for nearly a decade. Jon and I first crossed paths back in 2011 when I interviewed him about the wonderful Yes *Union* box set, he was executive producer. It was there that I learned what a devoted fan Jon is of Yes, in every incarnation. We quickly established a friendship surrounding our favourite band, a friendship cemented by our mutual belief that Yes is more than one man; that it is the sum of all its parts. Today, as the band continues to play to devoted audiences around the world, our belief still rings true.

So, sit back, put on your favourite Yes album (*Drama*, anyone?), and enjoy an unprecedented dialogue with progressive rock's greatest band, courtesy of someone who knows.

Andy Burns is the bestselling author of Wrapped In Plastic: Twin Peaks (ECW Press, 2014) and This Dark Chest of Wonders: 40 Years of Stephen King's The Stand (Cemetery Dance, 2018). By day he is the Digital Content Editor for SiriusXM Canada, and by night he runs the pop culture website, Biff Bam Pop!. Throughout his career Andy has interviewed Yes members Jon Anderson, Chris Squire, Alan White, Geoff Downes, Billy Sherwood and Jon Davison.

∿

Let's Talk... An Introduction
2013 & 2019

The year 1968 was an important year musically for a great many reasons. The Beatles recorded *The White Album*, the Stones recorded *Beggars Banquet*, and The Who began work on their rock opera *Tommy*. At the end of the same year, Cream split up and tucked away on the bill of their farewell concert at the Royal Albert Hall, whose opening act was a new band with a small name: YES. Whilst the name may well be small, the original idea for the name came from guitarist Peter Banks, who believed that the name would have to be printed big on the posters advertising concerts. He was right. Yes, of course, would go on to become one of the biggest rock bands in the world, and as I wrap up work on this book in 2013, the band are set to celebrate their 45th Anniversary. At the time of the Albert Hall concert, the band had been building up a very good reputation as a live act. Shortly thereafter, they signed a recording contract with a major label, Atlantic Records, who released their self-titled debut album the following year. Yes were to stay with Atlantic for the next 19 years and release some of the most exciting and challenging music of the 70s and 80s. Along the way, the band dropped members and changed line-ups, and of course, some of these changes were more contentious than others.

This "Perpetual Change" continues to this day, with the band recording their most recent studio album *Fly From Here* without the original singer, Jon Anderson. The changes didn't stop there either. The band changed the line-up again shortly after the European leg of the tour to promote the album with their then current vocalist leaving to make way for Jon Davison. Who is to say that there won't be more changes along the way before Yes finally play their last concert? Eighteen members have passed through their ranks in the band's 45-year history. Sometimes I think it is the very fact that the band have evolved and changed line-ups so often that they are still here making music in the 21st century. Whatever the reasons for each change, it stimulates and sparks creativity within the band. Nor is it a one-way trip, as the changes have also seen various ex-members return to the fold, and currently Geoff Downes is enjoying his second stint behind the keyboards with Yes. Jon Anderson, Steve Howe, and Rick Wakeman have all been in and out of the group at various times, and while Alan White has steadfastly held it all together on drums for the last 41 years, only Chris Squire has been a constant from the day he first met Jon Anderson and decided to form a band together.

My connection with Yes came in late 1972 when footage of the band performing at The Rainbow Theatre in London was featured on a British rock television programme called The Old Grey Whistle Test. This programme entertained and educated many young people's musical tastes in the UK through the 70s, and as I recall, the piece of music I saw was "And You And I." In short, I was hooked. From there, it was but a short time before I was collecting anything I could find relating to Yes. Fast forward many years later, I found myself in the radio industry presenting programmes for local Independent radio. This allowed me to present a rock show and, of course, interview various artists, including the members of Yes. I have also been incredibly lucky (not to say honoured) to have worked with the band on both group and solo album projects, including archive albums and DVDs.

This book contains many transcripts of my interviews with the various members of Yes throughout the years, talking about aspects of the band's history and various solo projects. I was also lucky enough to be able to talk to photographer Phil Franks, who took the photographs for the cover of *The Yes Album*. I can still recall the circumstances in which specific interviews took place, including the Geoff Downes interview covering the *Drama* period. I was accompanying Asia on their world tour in 2002, and the interview took place on the tour bus in Switzerland before the band played a gig to a massively enthusiastic audience. The lengthy Chris Squire interview covering the career of Yes took place in Chris' apartment in Chelsea, following the filming of a video interview for the reissue of *Fish Out Of Water*. Other interviews have taken place over the phone, such as the recent interviews with Tony Kaye about his time with the band, or Bill Bruford's account of the *ABWH* and *Union* periods, as well as lengthy but hugely entertaining interviews with Patrick Moraz about the *Relayer* album and its supporting tour.

All the interviews have one thing in common however: the musicians present their own take on the time they spent with this long-lasting, much loved, and astonishingly influential British rock band. This book does not set out to be the definitive story of Yes. As these interviews have taken place over many years, the opinions and recollections of those being interviewed may have changed, or even conflict with those of other musicians. It is quite common for musicians to be very enthusiastic about current releases or concerts, only to reflect later how things might have been done differently. Sometimes something may not have moved in quite the direction they had hoped, and consequently, look back differently in hindsight. I'm sure we all find our opinions about the music we like (and many other things in life) change or mellow over time, but then surely that is how it should be. The difference for me is that I don't have an album being subject to scrutiny by thousands (and in the case of some Yes albums, millions) of people over many years, or have my thoughts continually transcribed for people to read years later. But it does remain interesting to read these opinions and see how the material was viewed at any particular moment, and it also inspired the title of this book: *Time And A Word: The Yes Interviews*. Very few, if any, of these interviews, have ever been published before (certainly not officially!) and only a small number have been heard as part of radio broadcasts or on DVD. When I was reading them again with the distance of time, I was actually surprised by how honest and interesting these interviews actually are, and also the passion that comes across from all the members of the band. For that, I thank all the musicians, past and present, and also hope that you, the Yes Fan, enjoys reading these interviews. Perhaps they will spark memories for you as they do for me.

All that remains is for me to thank the many people who have helped or inspired me along the way, either with the interviews or the production of this book, including: Jon Anderson, Chris Squire, Peter Banks, Tony Kaye, Bill Bruford, Steve Howe, Rick Wakeman, Alan White, Patrick Moraz, Geoff Downes, Trevor Horn, Trevor Rabin, Igor Koroshev, Billy Sherwood, Tom Brislin, Benoit David, Oliver Wakeman, Jon Davison, Billy James, Sharon Chevin, Carlton Sandercock, Peter Noble, Dorothy Howe, Dave Clarke, Scotland "Scotty" Squire, Xilan Squire, Gigi White, Phyllis Moraz, Martine Dorey, Ron Devivo, Bob Hagger, Clive Bayley, John Anthony, Phil Franks, Roger Dean, Alan Fennah, Holly Quibell, Tom Wallace, Doug and Stephanie Curran, Don Rogers, Gillian Williams, Michael Flynn, Tom Matlosz, Chris Dean, Rob Fennah, Jane Druda, Mireille Druda, Lisa Druda, "Sonny", Graeme West, Jamie West, Rachel West, Aimee, and Grace.

I would also like to thank the following people who have supported me one way or another in all of this, and they are (in no particular order as they are all important!): Trevor Hughes, Daniel Earnshaw, Martin Darvill, Gordon Giltrap, Henry Potts, Paul Irons, Terry Underhill, Kevin Howard, Helen Anderson, Alison Jackson, Jos Heijmans, Malcolm Birkett, John Light, Larry Morand, Gene Aldridge, John "JP" Popwell, Harold Houldershaw, Kevin Roberts, Mark Jones, Alan Hewitt, George Mizer, Benito De Juan Dolio, and the late Phil Easton. Also, Lucretia Borgia, who supported me through a very difficult period in my life.

Finally, my Mum, the late Jean West, who surprised me when I first mentioned Yes, all those years ago, by knowing who they were and more importantly, who was in the band. I was so impressed back then, and I am still impressed, more than 40 years later.

Mum, this one is for you with much love. I miss the Dialogue we shared.
Jon Kirkman, England, August 2013.

The above introduction was written just before the publication of the first edition of my book on Yes. Many things have happened since that time, including a second large format of the book called *Dialogue* (2017). As with everything in life, there have been changes in the lives of the members of Yes and, of course, most of us who follow the band around the world. Changes both great and small, not least the tragic loss of founding member Chris Squire in 2015. Something that Chris Squire suggested in 2006 also came to pass: two versions of the band on the road, with Yes and Yes featuring Anderson, Rabin, Wakeman in 2018. Yes were also inducted into the Rock n Roll Hall of Fame in 2017. The band continues to this day, and in 2018 they celebrated their 50th Anniversary. In 2019, Yes released a triple vinyl album to celebrate that tour. Yes, as it currently stands, comprises of Steve Howe, Alan White, Geoff Downes, Jon Davison, and Billy Sherwood. There are plans for another studio album, and Yes are seemingly set for another 50 years. Contained in the first of a series of books, you will find interviews with members of Yes, both past and present, talking about Yes and their projects away from the band. I present to you, *Dialogue*.

Jon Kirkman, England, June 2019.

~

Dialogue
The YES interviews

Peter Banks: Beyond And Before
March 1998

Although Peter Banks was a founding member of Yes, his connections go further back to The Syn, where he was the guitarist alongside bassist Chris Squire. He was also briefly a member of the pre-Yes group Mabel Greer's Toyshop. Peter was the guitarist on the first two Yes albums (*Yes* and *Time And A Word*), although he was not overly pleased with the end result of the *Time And A Word* album, feeling that his guitar parts were sometimes submerged under the orchestration.

Peter was fired from the band in April 1970 and briefly joined Blodwyn Pig before forming his own band Flash. With Flash, he went on to record three well-received albums and relocated to Los Angeles. In March 1998, Peter was behind the archive album *Something's Coming: The BBC Recordings 1969-1970*, a double album that featured Yes in various sessions for the BBC, with the majority of the material coming from Peter's own archive. During the following interview, Peter discusses the Yes sessions and his post-Yes career.

Jon Kirkman (JK): At the moment, we have an album out that is going back a fair few years since you had a lot to do with it. The Yes album that is coming out at the moment is *Something's Coming*, is it?

Peter Banks (PB): We have walked past a lot of water under the bridge since those days, from 1969-1970.

JK: Let's talk about some of the stuff that you have done since leaving. For a lot of people, since you left Yes in 1970, until quite recently, you had literally disappeared. What have you been doing in the last 26 or 27 years or so?

PB: Well, I have literally disappeared! (*Laughs*) No, after Yes, I had a band called Flash, which was 1972. We only lasted two years; we broke up in 1974 in a traditional rock and roll style in Albuquerque, New Mexico. Pure Spinal Tap, it was! We were having a few disastrous gigs and that night I quit the band in the hotel and then I re-joined at 4am after a lot of soul searching. Then the band went home back to London. Flash was pretty interesting – we did three albums. I did my first solo album, and that was all in the space of two years. We were productive and most of our – I wouldn't say success – following was in America.

JK: Do you think that had a lot to do with the fact that you were an ex-member of Yes at that time?

PB: Yeah, and I hated all that. I went out of my way to avoid any questions – being young and naïve and big-headed. Any comparisons between Flash and Yes were strictly vetoed. But most of the reviews drew direct comparisons, which with critical hindsight was wholly appropriate.

JK: You had a big hand in the initial Yes sound, and Tony Kaye plays keyboards on the original Flash album, doesn't he? It is a fair comparison to make, isn't it?

PB: I went out of my way to deny any comparison whatsoever. At the time, when the band and I parted, and I put Flash together, I did not listen to any Yes material at all. I became a little fanatical about the whole thing, which with hindsight, was rather silly because it was my previous band. At the time, I wanted nothing to do with it.

JK: More recently, you have issued two or three solo albums for a small label [HTD]. Your first one – and don't take this the wrong way – reminds me of Jeff Beck's guitar workshop in the sense that on some tracks, there is like a collage over which you play sound effects and things like that.

PB: To be honest, I don't know. I do still go out of my way to not listen to other guitar players because in general, I am not very interested in what other people are doing with the guitar. Even at my ancient age, I'm still concerned I may steal a couple of links, or something will rub off on my style. Comparisons are fine, but they don't really mean much to me.

JK: Moving back to the Yes albums, what was it like listening to those albums and getting them ready for release? Did it bring back any good memories?

PB: No, it is a bit like going through old photo albums or looking at school photos and wondering why you look so silly, with silly hairstyles or whatever. It is nostalgia, that's all it is, and it is nice to indulge on occasion. In retrospect, the album doesn't sound as bad as I thought it would. I have obviously heard these BBC things before, and all I used to listen for was the mistakes, and most musicians would do that. Immediately when you have finished your new CD, you wish you could do it again, and it would sound much better. With a bit of distance, it is like dusting off an old scrapbook, and then I think it isn't so bad.

JK: To a lot of people, Yes means a very polished sound. But listening to the early Yes album, and indeed listening to this album, they were a really raw rock band at the time. I mean, they really went for it!

PB: Yes, no time for polishing at the BBC. It was a three-hour session, and you would be in and out with another band waiting to come in. I said in my sleeve notes to this CD that you were really under a lot of pressure. I think it was a three-hour session; it might have been three and a half hours. I think we got paid £15-25, a lot of money in 1969. You had to do three or four pieces in that amount of time, and we weren't even allowed to listen. We had guys saying to us, "That's fine; let's do the next one." That is the way it was. That is why it sounds raw and rough because it was.

JK: At the time Yes were getting underway, it was very much an albums market and singles were frowned upon. We are going to play a track now called "Sweet Dreams." I am not sure if that was a single for Yes, but it could have been. There was always that commercial edge, wasn't there? Even though some of the songs, like the cover versions, have been literally turned on their head.

PB: That was Jon, he loved the Beatles. Well, we all loved the Beatles, and Jon always had an ear for a catchy melody. It was never imposed upon us. We could have turned "Sweet Dreams" into a 20-minute epic, and I would have loved it. The only constraints we had upon us were our own, but they always had that catchy little edge. It was done deliberately, but not for the marketplace. In those days, we didn't even know about the business. We just wanted it to sound good. So along with the long pieces, we threw in something short.

JK: You left Yes in 1970, which seems like a long time ago now. And more recently, you've had some solo albums out. Do you like working on albums like this? This is just you, isn't it? It isn't a group situation.

PB: I am getting a little tired of playing by myself, actually. I am supposed to be working on what is my fifth album. The last three I have done have been basically by myself, so you do get a lot of guitar. I have no aspirations to do any kind of singing whatsoever, so what I am doing is obviously guitar-based. For the next album I am working out, I am thinking of using a different approach and using other musicians – a very radical approach for me! Basically, the reason I did these solo albums was initially for my own amusement, really. I had so much material on tape, and I thought someone else might like to hear this. In general, they have worked out well.

JK: Looking ahead to the future, what sort of time frame are we looking at for more albums, and possibly a group project from you?

PB: I am trying to avoid doing another solo album on my own. As far as working with other musicians, I am hoping to put something together for this summer, which, if that works out, will be terrific. I know the guys I want to use, and they want to work with me, but it is really a question of trying it out and seeing how it sounds. I much prefer playing live because I am much more of a spontaneous player. I am basically an improviser, and once I commit a guitar solo to tape, I am stuck with it, and a couple of months later, I end up hating it. Then a year later I might think that it is not so bad. I still record very spontaneously, but the way I record is very primitive and very basic. I have a very basic setup at home, and so I have to plan ahead what I am going to do and what piece is going to go where. I do miss the interaction and the immediacy of putting things down. Playing live is a whole different cup of tea. It is far more satisfying, and if anybody makes mistakes – fine, so be it, it is not a problem.

Peter continued to record solo albums and oversaw the re-issue of his debut solo album, which was re-issued along with the Flash albums. He also played sessions and remained in contact sporadically with Chris Squire and Jon Anderson. Shortly before his death, Peter intended touring America with members of the band Ambrosia. The set would have included mainly Yes songs that Peter had been involved with on the first two Yes albums. He was described by many as the "architect of Progressive Rock," and his contribution cannot be underestimated. Sadly, Peter passed away on March 7th, 2013, at his home in London, England.

∿

Chris Squire: Yesstory
November 2006

In late 2006, I was approached to film an interview with Chris Squire for what would become the deluxe edition of Chris' first solo album *Fish Out Of Water*. Following the filming of the interview, which was subsequently released as part of the deluxe package in 2007, we sat down to talk about Yes.

Jon Kirkman (JK): I have spoken to a lot of the guys in Yes over the years, yourself included, a few times, and what I wanted to ask was: you were in The Syn band in 1967, which was the sort of psychedelic era, and then Yes came about in 1968. In between The Syn and Yes was Mabel Greer's Toyshop. How long did that particular band last, because there were links between Yes and The Syn, wasn't there?

Chris Squire (CS): Well, there were, actually. At the end of The Syn's illustrious career, I ran into these guys, Clive Bailey, who was the guitar player, and I really can't remember the drummer's name, which is not very good of me [Martin Adelman]. They also had a bass player, so they had a three-piece band, and they were largely expressionist kind of players in that flower-power kind of way. The actual level of musicianship wasn't terrific, but they had a lot of ideas, especially Clive. He was a good ideas man, but not much of a guitar player.

I just kind of hooked up with them and it was around the time when people were experimenting with all kinds of drugs and music. We played the UFO, Middle Earth, and all the clubs that were around central London, which were places to go and have a jolly good time. What happened then was during the course of playing with them, I was never sure whether it was seriously going anywhere, you know. We played a few colleges, and we did a half an hour version of "Light My Fire" to end the show with a long guitar solo. I met Jon Anderson at that time, and Jon actually came along and sang with Mabel Greer's Toyshop at a couple of shows. That was really the beginnings of Yes, and the drummer fell by the wayside at a certain point. Clive Bailey was involved in some of the writings of the songs that were on the first Yes album, "Beyond And Before" being one, and during the course of the early Yes rehearsals, Peter Banks came in, who had been in The Syn. He came in and took over the guitar playing from Clive Bailey. So yeah, there is a tenuous link there. It is hard to say whether it was a very serious project or not – there was a lot of having fun involved in that band!

JK: Some of the material on the first Yes album was incredibly intricate. There were all sorts of different styles being brought to bear, and of course, cover versions. That wasn't particularly innovative at the time, as there were lots of bands travelling down that road. One of the big noticeable bands doing covers at the time was Vanilla Fudge, not that I am comparing them with Yes, but you took songs and made them your own which, particularly in the sense of doing, say, a Beatles song. It is very hard to put your own stamp on a Beatles song because it is a Beatles song. However, you managed to do that incredibly well.

CS: Not only did Yes end up recording "Every Little Thing," which is probably the song you are talking about on our first album but prior to that on our live show we did "Eleanor Rigby" and "I'm Only Sleeping." But I don't think they ever got recorded, even at the John Peel session. So, we did three Beatles songs, and maybe there was one more, but we definitely did those. Yes also covered stuff from *The Magic Garden* album, which was full of Jimmy Webb songs including that particular song. There were quite a lot of cover versions of Fifth Dimension songs, "Something's Coming" from West Side Story; an eclectic little band, we were.

JK: The first album came out, and it did quite well critically. You played with Cream at the Farewell Concert at the Albert Hall, and these were pretty high-profile gigs. If you compare the first album with the second album, the move forward was incredible! It was a very big leap. There was also an orchestra on that album, and I know some fans are still divided to this day about that. Parts of it are very good, particularly on the Richie Havens song, which I always get wrong, so I am not even going to try and remember it. I always get it the wrong way around, but that is an incredible song.

CS: Yeah, "No Experience Necessary" is what we used to call it. That happened because the first album just named *Yes* had a lot of our ideas. Jon and I were both very into listening to classical compositions and poppy ones like the Planets Suite and the New World Symphony and stuff like that, and Stravinsky we liked a lot. I guess we just made that leap for *Time And A Word*. We got in an arranger, Tony Cox, and had some orchestrations done. Not everyone in the band was happy with that. I can tell you that traditionally guitar players are never happy when the string players come along because they think they are stealing their thunder or something. It seems to be dyed in the wool that all guitar players I have come across are like that. So, Peter Banks did not really agree with the direction on that, and hence at the end of the recording of that album we parted ways. Anyway, that turned out very well, and Tony Colton, who was responsible for producing the album, was also the lead singer in a band called Heads, Hands, and Feet – quite a well-known band around London clubs in those days. We had got to know him, and somehow he ended up producing the album at Advision Studios on the homemade desk they had in there. The maintenance guys had made this desk, and Tony Colton decided he was going to mix the whole album on headphones because Blood, Sweat and Tears had come out, and everyone was saying that the effects were incredible.

So, I plugged the headphones into the desk. The headphone socket in the desk had a severe lack of bass on it. It was a very tinny sounding headphone socket, but nobody knew that at the time. I remember sitting at the back of the room with Steve Howe, who was actually at the mixing sessions for *Time And A Word*, even though he had not played on the album. Tony Colton was sitting there and Eddie Offord, the engineer, was sitting next to him, and he kept waving his hands asking for more bass. And of course, Steve Howe and I were listening to the mix through a couple of monitors. Steve Howe turned to me and said that the bass was getting awfully loud in the mix. I said, "I know, but he is the producer though, he must be good!" (*Laughs*) The weird thing was when that album came out, it got all these five and a half star reviews from the audio magazines for sound, and the bass was really, really loud on it. That was what kind of made me famous – this dodgy headphone socket! By the time we came to do *The Yes Album*, Eddie Offord was having to turn the bass up because of all the critical acclaim he had got on the previous album.

JK: You actually did one concert at the Royal Festival Hall with an orchestra, but you never repeated that particular experiment until *Magnification* quite some years later. Was it that bad of an experience for you guys at that time?

CS: It was actually at the Queen Elizabeth Hall, which is part of the Festival Hall complex. But this is going back to when we were using cloakroom coat rails to shore mikes off and dangle them above the violinists. It was very Heath Robinson in the days of miking up an orchestra. I don't know if anyone was ever there who could let us know what it sounded like, but I doubt if it was that balanced between the band and the orchestra.

JK: As you have already mentioned, Peter Banks left, or was sacked, depending on which story you want to believe – there have been a lot of them doing the rounds over the years. But he was the first in the band to go, which is always something that happens. You moved on, Steve Howe came in, and you made one album, *The Yes Album*, which again was another big step forward. Shortly after that, poor old Tony Kaye had to vacate the scene. It seemed to me at the time that it wasn't a case of it being anything personal, it was just a case of, "We are just moving on and feel you would be happier doing something else and we want to bring someone else in." I might be wrong, but I don't think it ever got personal with Yes. Maybe it has got a bit personal since, but at the time, I think it was for very valid musical reasons.

CS: I can give you a slight inkling about what happened with the Tony Kate situation. Tony Kaye was a bit of a man about town. On our first tour of America, which was on the back of *The Yes Album*, I used to share a room with Bill Bruford, and the recently married Steve Howe was sharing a room with Tony Kaye. Of course, Tony Kaye was having a good time on the American tour, and I think Steve Howe was getting a little bit upset in the adjacent bed at some of the goings-on! (*Laughs*) I suppose things like that can have an effect on relationships down the line. That was something we should have been able to patch up, get separate rooms or something because in those days tours weren't that expensive. But at the end of the tour, it came to pass that Rick was showing up all over the place as being the keyboard wizard, and I happened to have a conversation with him. I was probably trying to see if I could sort out the problem between Tony and Steve and thought, *Well if this guy comes in, I might solve the problem.*

JK: There have been all sorts of stories doing the rounds since then that Tony Kaye has refuted, like he was only kicked out because he didn't want to play the Hammond, etc. You see stories like that, especially since the advent of the internet and think, *That's not how I remember it!*

CS: Tony Kaye always was and still is a very good Hammond organ player. That is an art in itself, which is pretty different. It is a bit like asking me to play string bass on the next album – I would give it a go, but it is not really what I do, you know. I have tried it too, and it really is not what I do! (*Laughs*) No, I have always admired people like Sting who can actually play the string bass, and I think that has a lot to do with having started with it, as I know he did of course. Believe me – it was more about the rooming list than anything else.

JK: Well, we have come to the period when Rick came into the band, and there were two very strong albums. The great thing about the 70s, especially with a band like Yes, was that the albums were coming out at a terrific rate. These days, some bands spend that long getting the drum sound, and here is Yes making two albums in the space of 18 months – and critically acclaimed at that! We've got *Fragile*, then the one all the fans constantly relate to – *Close To The Edge*. I guess as an artist, you don't have too much time to look back at this stuff until it is well in the past.

16

CS: It is true. We had approximately six weeks to make *Fragile* from the beginning to the end of the mix to do it in. We were getting very popular and being booked to tour, and we wanted to expand our studio time because we were realising the possibilities of the work in the studios. Working with synthesizers, we knew that all that stuff took a little more time if you wanted to get to the level where the Beach Boys were at. But traditionally, an album took a couple of weeks to make. Probably the first *Yes* album took no longer than that. We had just a six-week window to make *Fragile* between our touring schedule, and that's why there are only four band tracks on it. The others were individual contributions because we didn't have the time to rehearse any more and find more songs to fill the album out.

JK: *Fragile* was the album that spawned the hit single in America "Roundabout," which in an edited form, was taken from the album. They do that a lot in America; they do take singles and edit them. I know most famously the guys in Pink Floyd said the people from the record company came up to them and told them if they took a single from the album and edited it, it would make the album go through the roof. I guess that must have happened with Yes and *Fragile* once "Roundabout" started to hit the radio stations.

CS: Yeah, I remember us all being shepherded down to some midtown studio by somebody or other from Atlantic and saying, "Listen to this great edit of 'Roundabout,' it is going to be hot and one of the best 45 tracks we've ever had!" We were all very suspicious, and of course, we heard this edit and thought it was awfully boring. But they persuaded us it would make a difference. It sold *Fragile* very well. Yes has never had a bona fide number-one album in America. I think we have had about four number-twos, but never a number-one. Someone else that week was always selling more. We did have a number-one single in the 80s with "Owner Of A Lonely Heart." Maybe *90125* may have been number-one, but it was like, "Oh, number-two again," with *Fragile* and *Close To The Edge*.

JK: If you think of Yes, you don't really think of singles. In the 80s it was a different matter, but in the 70s you were the de rigour albums band. Albums like *Topographic Oceans*, *Close To The Edge*, and *Relayer* all cemented that reputation, if anything, didn't they?

CS: Yes, they did. And just to emphasise the point: the fact that Led Zeppelin refused to have any edits done, or even have any promotional singles done, actually made them a bigger band because they had more of the college blue jean army behind them. They stuck to that and didn't go commercial, as it were. So, this guy who persuaded us that "Roundabout" would give us more sales – I'm not sure if it did more harm than good. That was the way it was then.

JK: I can't think of anything from *Close To The Edge* that you could edit out. Maybe that's wrong. You could get an edit out of "Close To The Edge," or possibly "And You And I," but *Topographic Oceans* – you would never get a single edit out of that!

CS: I don't think anyone tried with that. There was an edit of "Close To The Edge" called "Total Mass Retain," which was the second verse and a chorus. It wasn't really what should be known as a single, and once again, I don't really think it helped very much being out there. With *Topographic*, I don't think anyone ever attempted anything.

JK: With Yes, I think rather than looking at a small part, the band always wanted you to look at the big picture. This was a big piece of music; you wouldn't chop down Beethoven's Fifth, would you? That's a little bit pretentious, but it makes the perfect point, doesn't it?

CS: We were dealing with longer forms of music, and that is what we wanted to be known as doing. By the time we got to the mid-80s and did "Owner Of A Lonely Heart," which was a purposely-built single – and it did work as a single – nothing we had done in the 70s had lent itself to that format. In many ways, it is much more difficult to make a three and a half minute song than a 20-minute-long thing that has a lot of movements and complicated bits.

JK: There is an irony, though. In the late 70s at the height of punk when people were saying that bands like Yes were over, you had your biggest hit single in this country. It was a Top 10, three-minute song from the album *Going for the One* – "Wondrous Stories." This is the ultimate irony in the middle of this firestorm called Punk.

CS: Funnily enough, that song is going out next year as the main song for Cadillac, believe it or not. It is some new Cadillac they've got with an iPod carport for iTunes; something that hooks up for all your portable devices. They are using "Wondrous Stories" as the song behind the advert for Cadillacs. Who would have thought that?

JK: When Bill Bruford left, you were very surprised that he left the band. This is no reflection on Bill because he is a wonderful musician and a great drummer, but I felt there was a definite shift in Yes when Alan White came in. Certainly live, Yes became a little more rock and roll. Would you agree with that?

CS: As far as I was concerned, it was great to have played with two very different drummers, and I was able to walk around in different styles. But there is no doubt about it – Bill Bruford's playing was almost diametrically opposite to Alan White's. Bill led with his snare drum and used his bass drum for accents in a jazz-influenced way, whereas Alan came, as we all know, from the simplicity of playing "Imagine," just very straight rock and pop drums, and so a completely different drummer. Alan and I have been playing together for years, but we still call him the new boy, even though he joined in 1972! We have had 34 years of playing with each other. As I have said, it was great for me. Alan's organic style dictated the way Yes music went from then onwards. However, *Topographic Oceans* wasn't a straightforward pop sort of album, so it was probably good that he was there to ground it a bit, is all I can say.

JK: *Topographic Oceans, Close To The Edge*, and *Relayer* you have mentioned. Certainly, in the case of *Topographic Oceans*, they were extended pieces. Nowadays, you see bands going out and performing entire albums from their catalogue. Would that be something that might interest Yes? I'm sure there would be a lot of fans who would love to hear *Topographic Oceans* in its entirety. I'm sure you have played the entire album because it puzzled me when I went to see you in Liverpool. I thought, *When are you going to play something I know?* I was only 14 at the time, so you will have to forgive me for my lack of musical knowledge.

CS: I think that what we probably didn't realise at the time was that we had already established in people's hearts a favourite piece of music of theirs. Whereas, we were focused on the next piece of art and painting the next portrait, in a way. We don't have to paint the portrait we painted last year again. We were acting more as organic artists trying to always do something new, and thinking that people would want to just see our new product. But of course, it doesn't work like that. People get attached to pieces of music. There was always a lot of controversy in the band and within the audiences about how wise it was to do four sides of *Topographic Oceans* as the whole tour opening with "Close To The Edge" as the warmup, you know, five 25-minute-long pieces of music. I did actually catch glimpses of people nodding off in the audience around side three, so we were definitely trying to do a cerebral type of rock show, as opposed to a bodily functional kind of dance type – excitement and celebration of music, from that point of view. We were trying to appeal to people's heads.

JK: The album that came after those extended piece albums was – and I use this phrase in its best sense – a back to basics album for Yes. There was the best of the long pieces like "Awaken" on there, and some very direct, hard-hitting songs like "Going for the One," and of course, the big pop hit "Wondrous Stories." That brought Yes back big-time in the UK. I remember at the time everyone was saying that you were back on track and that this is what we wanted. Even the music press, who had been a little dismissive of things like *Topographic* and *Relayer*, were back on side. Then with the next album, *Tormato*, they were back giving the band a really hard time.

CS: Well, Tormato was an interesting album. Once again, it had a variety of places the music was coming from. We were all writing and trying to get our bits on the album. There was "Release, Release," which was us really tipping our hat to Punk. It is a very aggressive, punkily-played type of song, even though it is musical as well. It definitely has got that element about it. Then there was "Future Times," which is kind of cool. It has got me playing the Mutron bass with effects all over the place, and Steve Howe and Rick Wakeman both seeing who could play more notes in a bar than the other one most of the time! (*Laughs*) That was also to do with the fact that Jon had begun to come into the studio for the first time and whack down the chords and play along on his acoustic guitar with the band. This made Steve and Rick want to play lead stuff all the time. Then Jon would go, "Oh, I'll just take my guitar out now." Then there would be this big hole in the middle, and there would be me and Alan and some guys fluttering away at the time. But in a way, it was kind of an invention in itself. Those tracks are interesting to listen back to.

One of the best songs I ever wrote was "Onward," which was a simple song. It was on that album, and I was very happy with that. Andrew Jackman did the arrangement on that. He was the chap who did the orchestration on *Fish Out Of Water*. He did pop in and out of the Yes history over the years to do little things with us. I wasn't sure what was going on with the album cover for *Tormato*. It wasn't Roger Dean; it was Po and Storm from Hipgnosis and this idea of a tomato. Then someone actually found a tor in Devon. I think it was Po, and it was actually called "Tor-Mato." We thought he was making it up, but there actually is one, and it kind of got Druidy again. Then we said, "Let's have this guy who looks like he is divining for water and let's smash a tomato on it." I don't think anyone had a concept of what the fucking sleeve should look like, so it went out like that. An interesting album, though. Jon has that interesting track on there, "Circus Of Heaven," which is me playing a bit of reggae, really, and interesting colours from the other guys on that – also "Silent Wings Of Freedom."

JK: I was going to say that one of the key tracks for me was "Silent Wings Of

Freedom." The other thing about the album was that it coincided with the 10th Anniversary of Yes. You went on this huge 10th Anniversary tour, and then the next thing we heard was that the band had split. Jon had left, and Rick had left with him. A lot of people thought that was it. You were very much the prime mover saying it wasn't over and that you could continue. You brought in Geoff Downes and Trevor Horn. I know one person at the time who was absolutely horrified. They wouldn't even listen to the album, which was a bit silly because if anything, *Drama* was one of the more Yes-sounding albums of the period. Although, it did presage a very contentious period for Yes. It is fair to say that it split the fan base, didn't it?

CS: What happened there was that Rick had been in and out of Yes, as he continues to do to this day. He does these "away" missions, as they call them in Star Trek. He tends to gravitate backwards and forwards. I guess Jon wanted to give that a go, because at the time he was, or was about to, or did do, a solo tour. I remember going to see him at the Albert Hall with his backing band, and I didn't quite know what to make of it, really. It sounded fine and everything, but it was just a bit odd to see. The bottom line of that is that both those guys felt the needed to go and do other things outside of the band. That left Alan, Steve, and I. We had already started rehearsing for the *Drama* album, although it wasn't that then. We had been rehearsing and had ideas for tunes, and what actually happened was that Geoff Downes and Trevor Horn had hooked up with Brian Lane, who was our manager at the time, mainly because they were both big Yes fans and they had both become hugely successful with "Video Killed The Radio Star." In fact, this had become the biggest selling single worldwide, or in the charts, for the longest number of weeks.

So, Brian lucked out because they loved Yes as musicians, and they ended up in our office just about the same time, so it was obvious. I said, "You play keyboards, you sing, obviously you know how to write a hit, do you want to come and join the band?" Of course, I had a tough job selling it to Steve Howe and Alan White as well, and I had the job of selling it to Jill Sinclair, who was Trevor's counterpart and his manager, to an extent. I had to persuade her that this would be good for Trevor to come and do it. There was a lot of work involved in pulling that line-up together, but the actual album came out pretty good, especially as once again, we were up against a big-time schedule and there were already tours booked in the States. There were four sold-out dates at Madison Square Gardens, and people thought Jon and Rick were still in the band when the tickets had been sold. So, we had to make this album and get the band speeded up to be able to go and play to the expectancy of the fans. It was a lot of long nights, and there was a lack of sleep during that period. But we did manage to pull it off, and *Drama* has got a quality about it that stands the test of time.

JK: I am a big fan of this album, but then I have never really disliked anything that Yes have done. Maybe I am in the minority, I am hoping I'm not, but certainly in the 80s there seemed to be a big division. It was either old-time Yes, or you wanted the band to move forward, and I'm into that, and yet *Drama* is the member of the family we don't speak about for some reason. I don't know why that should be. Musically, it should appeal to the fans that like the older style Yes, and also some of the songs should appeal to the newer fans.

CS: I had what I like to call "hipper" friends in New York, and I was friendly enough with them for them to give me an honest opinion. After they had seen the Madison Square Garden show with Trevor Horn and Geoff Downes, they were completely blown away, and it certainly kept the Yes reputation intact.

JK: I think the big problem was in England though, more than America. America were a little more open, I believe, to the *Drama* line-up. In England, there were in some cases outright hostility.

CS: I guess it's because Trevor and Geoff had been so successful with what was, let's face it, a pop song. It is a very good pop song that has stood the test of time, and one that we still hear today.

JK: I think Trevor had the hardest job though, replacing Jon Anderson. Geoff had it slightly easier because he was the fourth keyboard player down the line. Trevor, God bless him, had to stand at the front and pretend to be Jon Anderson for a lot of people, and some did not think he was up to it.

CS: It was a tall order, and I will always commend him on his bravery for doing that.

JK: If you look at Yes' entire catalogue, and now you can look back at 38 years of the band and recordings, you must be pretty satisfied. You can think, *Yes, as a body of work this hangs together*.

CS: Yes, it is a body of work. I am not sure the exact figure, I suppose we have probably sold something like fifty million albums including the repackaged versions over our career, which is pretty decent. I am just glad that we survived to be able to do it. I'm sure that there will be Yes shows with Rick, Jon, Steve, Alan, and myself that will be coming up this year [2007] or 2008.

There may be an alternative version of Yes as well if somebody doesn't want to work as much as others. We are having to figure out a new way of doing Yes shows.

JK: That is something I want to ask you. Again, it is down to the internet – the stories and rumour change hourly! But they are saying that the *90125* line-up is going to do something minus Jon. I have spoken to Jon, who says he can't do anything next year, but maybe the year after. You hear all these different stories. You mention an alternative Yes, so what exactly are you talking about?

CS: I am not absolutely sure. All these ideas are out there, and some of them are ideas that people think I have had, but I am actually getting them from somewhere else! They probably come with the tag of "Chris' idea," but this is not necessarily so. We may work with Trevor again in the future. He is so stuck into his movie career right now though, and I don't see him jumping off the gravy train that he is on very easily because he is doing so well at it. He has expressed interest in playing live again at some point. Whether it would be with or without Jon, I don't know. I really don't know. It is getting to that point now where you have to respect other people's wishes in the band, and if some people want to wind down their touring career, or the amount of shows that they are willing to do and other guys are willing to work more, we may have to have a kind of a "Come and see Yes as this, and if you're lucky, certain people will be there that night."

JK: One of the stories that seems to have found favour at the moment, and you have already done this with the *Union* tour and album is, why not do it as a one-off, film it, record it, a thing about the history of Yes? You get the original line-up to do a few songs, then Peter Banks drops out, and you do something from *The Yes Album*, etc. and work it through that. Maybe you could bring everyone on at the end to do a version of "Roundabout." That would be an interesting concept, thinking about the number of people who have been in Yes.

CS: I haven't heard that idea before, but it is not that unintelligent of an idea. It is something that may be worth thinking about. I need to make a note of all of these different ideas and then sit down and mark them like essays or something!

JK: You don't want to get into the idea of Yes by committee though, because that is just never going to work.

CS: I was going to add though, that when we did do the *Union* tour, fortunately for me there was only one bass player, and fortunately for Jon, there was only one lead vocalist, but there were varying degrees of difficulties for the other musicians who were playing the guitar, keyboards, and drums. But having said that, there are some live recordings of that, and for some ridiculous reason we, or whoever was promoting the tour, never recorded it. I have heard the bootlegs that are out there, and they do sound quite amazing. That particular larger-than-life Yes with the extra sound involved in having eight musicians on stage instead of five is very impressive. It is not beyond the possibility that one could go into that realm again. It would just have to be planned very well.

JK: If you were going to include everyone including Peter, Tony, Trevor, and so forth, planning would be everything. I have seen the DVD that came out on laserdisc in Japan of the *Union* tour, which is the Shoreline gig, and it was pretty good. That is something I think a lot of fans would be interested in. I guess a lot of fans would just like to see Yes back on the road and also doing an album, but it isn't just as simple as that and hasn't been that simple for a long time.

CS: One would like to think that things could be done as easily, but let's hope that we can pull something together that will be interesting.

JK: Well, I hope so, and I know that the massive fan base is there ready and waiting for whatever you want to do.

CS: That's great, thanks for that.

At the time of this interview in November 2006, Yes was on one of its regular breaks, although Chris did say that the band had plans to celebrate its 40th Anniversary in 2008. Sadly, events took over, and Jon Anderson was taken seriously ill and unable to take part in the planned tour. Chris, along with Steve Howe and Alan White however, pressed on and recruited Benoit David to replace Jon Anderson, and Oliver Wakeman came in to play keyboards. In 2011 the band released their latest album, *Fly From Here*, which was produced by Trevor Horn and also saw the return on keyboards of Geoff Downes. The summer of 2012 saw the band returning to the USA for more tour dates in the company of Procol Harum.

Also, at the time of this interview, Chris Squire recorded a solo album for the Christmas market, *Chris Squire's Swiss Choir*. One of the guests on the album was guitarist Steve Hackett, and it was at the sessions for Swiss Choir that the seeds were sewn for the Squackett project, which saw the collaboration reach fruition with the release of the album *A Life Within A*

Day in May 2012.

Strange as it may seem, however, Chris mentioned that there might very well be two versions of Yes, and in 2017, that very thing happened when Jon, Rick Wakeman, and Trevor Rabin added the name Yes to ARW, making it Yes featuring ARW.

~

Alan White: 40 Years With Yes
October 2012

Alan White celebrated his 40th Anniversary with Yes – the band he joined with just three days' notice in the summer of 1972 following Bill Bruford's departure from Yes to King Crimson. Since then, Alan has played on every single Yes album. Before Yes, Alan had played in several bands, including with Alan Price and also Terry Reid and Joe Cocker. In fact, he was drumming for Joe Cocker when he got the call to join Yes. It was his membership of the Plastic Ono Band that set Alan apart from many other drummers. Alan played on the Plastic Ono Band's *Live Peace In Toronto 1969* live album, as well as on John Lennon's "Instant Karma" single and the *Imagine* album. He also managed to play on the Yoko Ono album *Fly*, and George Harrison's *All Things Must Pass*. Throughout this interview, Alan discusses his time with Yes and how he came to be the second-longest member of the band since joining in June 1972.

Jon Kirkman (JK): 2012 is your 40th Anniversary year with Yes, but do you remember who it was that made the first contact with you? Because at the time, you were playing with Joe Cocker, which musically is a million miles away from Yes.

Alan White (AW): (*Laughs*) Yeah it was, but I do remember who made the first contact. It was Tony Dimitriades, who was my kind of business manager and was also the business manager of Eddie Offord as well. So he used to advise me on what I should do with any money I earned and stuff like that. He was more an acting manager, really. There was nothing written down formally, but Eddie, Tony, and myself were very good friends, and we even shared an apartment together when he first came out of law school. Eventually, of course, he went into management and earned a ton of money with Tom Petty (*laughs*).

So I was in Rome during the last night of the tour, and somebody told me that this guy had been trying to contact me desperately. Anyway, he called again and said, "You have to get on a plane in the morning and come back to England because Yes want you to join the band." I flew to England and I was staying with Eddie Offord at his apartment in Victoria, London and Chris Squire and Jon Anderson came around and we sat down and talked for a while and they said, "We've got a proposal," because I had actually already played with the band informally two weeks before. The band had been rehearsing, and I had gone down there to this rehearsal room, which was beneath some sewing shop in Shepherds Bush, and I remember it being very small. It was only about 20' by 20'. It was tiny, and all the equipment was in there, and I was in the corner like an innocent bystander. I had heard of them, of course. I heard of them when I was playing with Terry Reid, and I heard them in the clubs and said, "Who is that band?" I thought they were damned good, amazing, in fact. Anyway, I was only there with Eddie and just a guest, nothing more, and Bill, I think, was at that point trying to get out of the band and hook up with Robert Fripp and join King Crimson. Basically, they were rehearsing "Siberian Khatru" from *Close To The Edge*, and I had been playing stuff like that with my own band out in the country. But for some reason, Bill had to go somewhere – I didn't know what for – and when Bill left, rather than break up the rehearsal, Eddie said, "Well if you want to carry on playing, Alan doesn't mind jumping in with you." So I jumped in and started playing "Siberian Khatru." And the guys must have liked it because I just fitted in and played the song. And I think that must have made a mark, because just a couple of days later Chris Squire came to see me play with Joe Cocker at the Rainbow in London, and that is where they asked me, "Do you want to join the band?"

So I said, "Yeah, I'll give you three months and give myself three months to get adjusted to see how it goes with each other." And here I am now, 40 years later! (*Laughs*)

JK: How did you feel when you were asked to join? Were you aware of what was going on in the background and that Bill wanted to leave?

AW: No, I wasn't aware at all. I had no idea. I don't think anyone knew actually, not even Eddie. They recorded the album *Close To The Edge*, and then all of a sudden he told them he didn't want to carry on with the band, so he never actually played the material from *Close To The Edge* live at the time.

JK: Steve Howe told me that Bill had offered to do the tour, but Steve had said, "No. If you are going to go, then go now." So I guess like many things in the music business, it is the right place, right time. Would you agree?

AW: Oh yeah. Of course, there is a bit of that, definitely. But the shocker was that they told me they had a gig in Dallas, Texas in three days!

JK: That must have been a shock for you because the Yes setlist at the time was, I imagine, pretty involved. The music from *Close To The Edge* alone was very demanding, but the other material in the set couldn't have been easy.

AW: Well the song "Close To The Edge" was demanding, certainly. In fact, very demanding to play. I almost didn't sleep. I was listening to the music night and day, and I really drilled it into myself, to be honest. I did feel, though, that I was really quick at learning stuff. I just sat around and listened to the stuff and learned the arrangements. I don't really recall sitting down with everyone and playing it through, though. I just got on the plane and went and jumped in at the deep end! (*Laughs*)

JK: Do you think that served you well because you didn't have the time to sit down and think about what you were letting yourself in for then?

AW: (*Laughs*) Yeah. I think that was true for the band and me, really. But I did work damn hard to get to that point, and I think the band were more worried than I was that I was going to get everything right in front of ten thousand people. When we came offstage at the end of that first night, I remember Chris Squire saying to me, "Well, you played everything great, but it wasn't that great a show, but we got through it." So the first few nights were really just a case of me honing myself into it, and by the fourth or fifth gig, we were up and running, and it started feeling really good.

JK: Although you gave each other three months, something must have been right, because the tour went on for seven months eventually.

AW: Yeah. It went on and on, and we got a show down, and it was a pretty damn good show, as you can hear on *Yessongs*.

JK: The American tour was a big step in itself, but the very first British concert – and the launch for the *Close To The Edge* album – was at Crystal Palace. Surely you must have felt a little apprehensive about that concert, as the press was bound to be there.

AW: Well, by that time, I had done quite a few gigs with them, so I was a little more confident by then. It wasn't as daunting as the American leg, obviously.

JK: Home country gig though… Sure the pressure was on a little…

AW: Well yeah, the home crowd and everything. And the press was there, as you say, and they were just starting to get a big reaction in the UK. In fact, it was starting to get kind of big-time back home at that point.

JK: You said during the tour you had recorded *Yessongs*…

AW: Yeah, and that was kind of unfair really because I hadn't been in the band that long. But for some reason, a lot of people love that album.

JK: I think that is because it's considered by many Yes fans to be the definitive live Yes album. There have been a few more live albums since then, but when you sat down and listened to *Yessongs*, did you think it was okay, or were you hearing things you wanted to do better?

AW: Well, it wasn't that well recorded, actually. I thought the playing was good and the band played really well, even though some of the songs were a little overplayed and rushed on stage, but live albums are a little bit like that, and you just have to take that in your stride. It was recorded well enough for a live album, but nowadays, of course, it is totally different. But it could have been a little better sonically, I think, but it was what it was – the way old vinyl sounds.

JK: What I think is special about it – and I am talking about both the album and the film – is that it captures the moment, and that can't be bad as a piece of documented history.

AW: Yeah. Well, it captures almost a virgin moment for me with the band and sees me finding my way still.

JK: Well that was where I first got into the band, with that film, and so for me, this year is my 40th Anniversary following the band. The song that hooked me was "And You And I," and I am sure you hear similar stories all over the world.

AW: Well, that is a great song when it's played properly; there are lots of different movements in it. It is very Yes-like in terms of the anthems, and it is a good song.

JK: So after the tour then, it was time to do another album. But this wasn't going to be just any old album – and Steve and Jon took the bull by the horns and came up with the concept for *Tales From Topographic Oceans*.

AW: Well, that took a hell of a lot of time, but it was Jon and Steve with a hell of a lot of input from everyone else. We were in Manticore down in Fulham – which was an old cinema that ELP had bought and turned into a studio and rehearsal facility – and we were in there for three months working on it and rehearsing it. And it was really intensive because we only took one day off a week at weekends. We worked over eight hours a day on that just getting it right. So that was how long we took to get it right before we even took it to the studio.

JK: Were you aware of the writing sessions that Jon and Steve undertook on the tour? Wasn't most of it written in various hotel rooms in America during the American tour?

AW: I'm not so sure about that. I think there were writing sessions in hotel rooms on tour, but a lot of it in terms of piecing it together, the rhythm section, and the whole thing of stitching it together, took place at Manticore. For instance, Side Three is mostly instrumental. There is not much in the way of vocals on it, so there was a hell of a lot of work done down at Manticore piecing it together. But when we got to the studio, we recorded it in so many small pieces, which were then all edited together.

JK: It was recorded in Morgan studios, wasn't it?

AW: Yeah. Morgan Studios in North London.

JK: Were you a party to the discussions as to where the album should be recorded? I believe half the band wanted to record in the country and half the band wanted to record in the town.

AW: Well, it was one of those things at the time, really. People lived in the country and wanted to record there, but I felt Morgan was good enough to get all the backing tracks done. There were really crazy stories around that time when Jon said the song didn't sound as good as when he sang it at home in the bathroom, so he had the roadies build a shower cubicle for him in the studio with real ceramic tiles so he could sing in that! (*Laughs*) There was a lot of crazy stuff like that going on back then, I can tell you!

JK: I believe there were hay bales in the studio as well to give a rustic atmosphere to the studio.

AW: Yeah, there were hay bales in the studio… And Rick brought in two bloody life-size cardboard cows that he stuck in the corner of the control rooms! It looked like a barnyard! That's how long we were in there and how bored Rick was getting at the time because it really wasn't his favourite album at all.

JK: He said he had to have his keyboards professionally cleaned because they were full of dust mites and insects. How did you feel about all this? It was the first album you recorded with the band, and all this madness is going on around you. Even looking back over 40 years, this is one strange recording session!

AW: I tell you what… I don't think anyone could recall vividly all the mad moments that went on in there at the time! There was something every day that was just so off the wall it was ridiculous! (*Laughs*)

JK: How did you feel about the general concept of the album then?

AW: Oh, I was totally getting into it, yeah. I was totally into all these new rhythms Chris and I were getting into, just new stuff. It was pretty adventurous. There were all sorts of different time signatures and everything, so it kept me happy.

JK: That album was very rhythmic and percussive in parts as well, I think.

AW: Yeah, we did all kinds of stuff. But that drum solo at the end of "Ritual" took a while to pull together and get the whole thing down, and even to teach the whole band to play the drums. I always remember trying to get Steve Howe to play the drums, but he kept saying, "It hurts my hands." He played timbales live for a while on that section, but he said, "I can't play the guitar after playing the drums," So I just said, "Well why don't you just sit out of that, and the rest of us will play the drums?" (*Laughs*)

JK: I remember seeing you live on that tour, and you opened up with "Close To The Edge" and then played *Topographic Oceans*. So what was it like taking *Topographic Oceans* out on the road?

AW: Yeah, "Close To The Edge" was the rock song… (*laughs*) But bringing it bang up to date, we are going to be doing something similar on the tour next year by playing three albums on the next tour in their entirety, starting with *Close To the Edge* then *Going For The One*, and then taking a short break and then playing *The Yes Album* at the end. It's the new thing, really. A lot of bands are doing a themed tour playing a certain album from their catalogue in its entirety, and the public seems to like the fact that a band will play an album all the way through.

JK: But you were doing that with Yes 40 years ago.

AW: Yeah, started a trend, I guess. But when we were doing things like *Topographic Oceans*, we started getting reviews saying, "I don't believe they played the whole album." If we were going to play *Topographic Oceans* in full now, I think it would probably take us a couple of months to rehearse that now! (*Laughs*)

JK: Are you surprised by how highly regarded albums like *Topographic Oceans* and *Relayer* are these days? Because if you read the reviews at the time, some critics would have you believe that the albums weren't regarded at all, never mind highly regarded.

AW: Well the press thought we were crazy, but I have to hand it to Atlantic Records who let us record and release albums like that back then. A lot of record companies would just say, "Hang on a minute. We can't market or sell that," but Atlantic just let us get on with it, and *Topographic Oceans* still sells today.

JK: After the tour was over, then you were looking to make what became *Relayer*, and yet Rick wasn't really keen if it was going to be anything like *Topographic Oceans*. And of course, hindsight tells us it wasn't really like *Topographic Oceans*, but Rick decided to leave as he felt he couldn't continue with the band.

AW: Well, what happened was that we did a gig, and after the gig, he left the band. He just said, "This is not what I want to be doing really," which left us up in the air, really. We tried a few people out to replace Rick. Did you know we tried out Vangelis? That was a scary day! (*Laughs*)

JK: Patrick told me he actually auditioned on Vangelis' keyboard rig and what he played at that audition ended up on *Relayer*. So the feeling within the band must have been a positive one towards Patrick?

AW: Yeah, it was pretty instant. And he did audition for us using Vangelis's rig, which was still set up, and yeah it was very good. He came in and really impressed us – he was a great keyboard player.

JK: I'm going to throw a rumour into the conversation now because there are all sorts of rumours around a band like Yes...but Chris has said it could happen, apparently. But the rumour is that you are going to do something on Broadway, and maybe Patrick could come and guest on something if you do that.

AW: Yeah, well, there are always loads of ideas floating around, and we have been tossing this idea around. And to be honest, it came up a while ago, and some of the people in the business have said we would be committing financial suicide doing something like that. But you look at the bands that do that, and it is basically getting the audience to come to you, and you put on a spectacle. But a lot of bands who try that do fall flat on their face, so I'm not sure really about that. But there is still something about going to see a band when it comes to your town that people like. I don't know...at the moment that idea is still on hold, but it could happen.

JK: I would like to move onto 1975 and 1976. Yes were probably one of the biggest rock bands in the world at that point. You were playing big arenas and even football grounds in the UK and stadiums in America. Your contemporaries at this point would have been Led Zeppelin, The Who, and The Rolling Stones.

AW: We were very big then, that's for sure, but we were like the oddballs out of all those bands you just mentioned. Led Zeppelin and The Who had a more "rock star" image than we did. I would say that Yes were kind of the second stream though after those bands who were all playing stadiums regularly.

JK: But you played at the JFK Stadium in Philadelphia.

AW: Well, we did play stadiums. We played one or two tours where there were some stadium dates in there, but we played a lot of arenas and that kind of level of gig.

JK: When you played Philadelphia, you played to over 130,000 people.

AW: I would still like to find the footage from that gig because somewhere someone has it. It was definitely filmed. I saw it once but have not seen it since and I can't trace it anywhere.

JK: Apparently you were being filmed by two guys from Canada with a view to releasing another film along the lines of *Yessongs II*. After it had been filmed, they showed Brian Lane the rushes of the film, and Brian Lane didn't like what he saw. According to Chris Squire, they disappeared with the film, and no one has seen or heard from them since.

AW: Actually I remember that story now, yeah, but I would love to see it again. It would be great if that surfaced again, particularly now. I remember there was a great helicopter shot over the crowd and I remember thinking it looked like a beehive. There were a lot of bonfires dotted around at the end of the night where they were trying to keep warm.

JK: Once the tour was over it was time for another album, but you had already started work on what was going to be *Going For The One* with Patrick, and then Rick came back into the picture.

AW: We had started working on *Going For The One*, you are right. But it didn't work out with Patrick, and when Rick heard the music we were doing, he said yes to coming back into the band, as he said the music sounded better to him than the music when he left.

JK: I think for me and many others, *Going For The One* is a great album because it manages to mix the longer songs like "Awaken" with shorter tracks like "Wondrous Stories."

AW: Well "Awaken" is one of my favourite Yes songs, really.

JK: That is the example of the longer song, although not as long as something from *Relayer* or *Topographic Oceans*, but when I mean short, I mean relative to other Yes songs, rather than a three-minute single.

AW: Well, short for us is usually six or seven minutes. I think that the actual track "Going For The One" is a pretty powerful track, particularly on stage, and "Turn Of The Century," which is not easy to play at all. And "Wondrous Stories," of course, was a massive hit in England. It was a big hit at the height of punk, and it was this kind of acoustic song.

JK: Tell me about *Tormato*, because for some Yes fans it is not a highly regarded album, particularly coming off the back of *Going For The One*, which was a big success commercially. Did you feel it was a good album at the time?

AW: I don't know…I have mixed feelings about *Tormato* these days. I will listen to one song we did and think, *Well that was pretty damn good*, and then I will listen to another one and think, *Wow that sounds like a bunch of crap*, so I kind of swing between one thing and another really, when it comes to *Tormato*.

JK: I like "Onward."

AW: "Onward" is a great track, and that is one that survives through to this day. We have played that recently, or fairly recently. It's a Chris Squire song, and in fact, Chris gets a lot of requests through his publishers by people who want to use it as a wedding march, believe it or not.

JK: That is a strange song to walk up the aisle to though.

AW: (*Laughs*) Yeah it is, really.

JK: How did you feel when Jon and Rick decided to leave during the sessions for the follow up to *Tormato*? Was it a shock?

AW: Well, there was Steve, Chris, and myself, and we thought, *Well, what do we do now?*

JK: I believe you broke your leg and that put a stop to proceedings.

AW: Oh yeah, well that really needed to happen because the music really wasn't that good. We were all raving our brains out...actually not so much raving our brains out, but we were totally disinterested in the songs we were working on. I remember saying, "These songs are not very good." I remember the Paris sessions, and we were recording. Rick is reading a book or a paper over in the corner, and there is Chris and myself working on something, and Jon had a separate little booth, which was halfway up the wall, and it had a glass window in it. And he is in there with a painting easel, painting pictures, and playing an acoustic guitar. We were recording a take with the red light on and everything, and we could hear this music coming down from Jon's booth, which was nothing to do with the song we were playing. It was Jon playing another song. It was total distraction everywhere, and nobody was listening or interested. So I call it a blessing that I broke my leg. Actually, it was Richard Branson that took me roller skating, and I said, "Are you sure this is okay, as I am halfway through an album," and he said, "No, it will be fine." And so we had a bottle of wine and went roller skating at one o'clock in the morning, and I fell over. And I didn't actually break my ankle – I just cracked it. But they put a cast on it, and it was my bass drum foot, so I couldn't play the drums. In fact, I couldn't do anything. Richard Branson fell over as well. In fact, he fell another six feet and slipped a disc, so we both hobbled out of the skating rink.

JK: What were your feelings on Roy Thomas Baker? Jon doesn't like to be drawn on this and be seen as pointing the finger or blaming anyone for anything, but I get the impression that although the band chose to work with Roy Thomas Baker, once the sessions started Jon was definitely not happy.

AW: I think, in reality, it was just that no one was into what we were doing. We were just going through the motions, living in Paris, and doing a tax year out of England while we recorded an album. And everyone was distracted by one thing or another, really. There was no focus at all as to what was going on, and we were spending way too much money. It cost an absolute fortune for us all to be there with apartments and the studio, and just everything, really. Sometimes it would be days before we got anything done.

JK: Do you remember the point after Jon and Rick left when Trevor Horn and Geoff Downes came into the picture?

AW: We went back to London, and there was just the three-piece with me, Chris, and Steve, and we were just sat around one day thinking, *Well, what do we do now?* These two guys are off doing their solo stuff, thinking they can do better, and they did do some great stuff. But at the same time, it wasn't Yes. So we were at a meeting, and I think it was actually me who said,

"I'm going to get the office to book Redan Recorders," which was a rehearsal facility in London, "And whoever turns up on Monday is in the band." It really was as simple as that. And that is what started the whole "Drama" period. We started rehearsing as a three-piece, and Trevor and Geoff were in the room next door, and they started coming in, and within a week they had moved in! (*Laughs*) They said they had a song for us and the next thing you know, we're writing *Drama*!

JK: Which I think is a really great Yes album, and in fact, better than *Tormato*.

AW: Yes, I think it is. In fact, it is way better than *Tormato* for me. "Machine Messiah" is a great song.

JK: "Tempus Fugit" is also a great song for me.

AW: "Tempus Fugit" and "Machine Messiah" are two of my favourite songs to play live.

JK: Did it feel strange going out on tour without Jon fronting the band?

AW: No, not really. It felt kind of natural, really. It felt new and like the band had new life in it, which of course with Trevor and Geoff in the line-up, it did. There was something very exciting about it, and everyone in the band jumped up, and the band started sounding great.

JK: I think it would be fair to say that it was received a little better in America than it was in the UK.

AW: Yeah, that's for sure. Geoff's a very good keyboard player, and he has very modern ideas about sounds, and that helps a lot. And of course, Trevor Horn has always been good with lyrics.

JK: When the *Drama* tour finished, there was a meeting where it was decided that you and Chris were going to go off and work with Jimmy Page. Trevor didn't want to do anymore – certainly not fronting the band at least – and that left Geoff and Steve, who did consider continuing with Yes at one point. But from your point of view, was that really as far as it could go with Yes?

AW: Well I don't know really, because for some reason Yes always had that thing about them whereby they always kept its head above water. But then when Steve and Geoff went off to Asia, Chris and I thought once again, *What do we do now?* Because at that point, we still owned the name. There was the two of us, and we owned the name, and I remember that perhaps it was the last tour, or maybe the one before that, where we were in the limo, and Brian Lane played us this cassette of a guy called Trevor Rabin. And I thought he was a pretty good guitarist, but left it at that until about 1981 or 1982 when Atlantic Records brought his name up again and suggested we meet him. Next thing we know, he is in London and the three of us go for a Chinese meal together, and we get on. So the next day, we went down to Chris's house for a jam and then decided to move it forward. Chris called Tony Kaye, and that was it.

JK: Both Chris and Trevor said when you did jam together, it was the worse jam ever, but you all got on great.

AW: Well, it probably was. In fact, it was all over the place. I think we'd had a few beers, to be honest, but yeah, we got on.

JK: It wasn't Yes though was it?

AW: No, we were going to be called Cinema.

JK: You split in 1980 and then came back in 1983. Nowadays, that would not be considered a long time between albums. In fact, some bands have taken that long to get a drum sound they like.

AW: (*Laughs*) Yeah, exactly! Well, it only became Yes when Jon came back on board, and he loved what he heard and wanted to sing on the album. And when he did, it sounded totally like a Yes album, so that is why the name reverted to Yes. It was a modern version of Yes. We spent six or nine months working on *90125*, and we had most of the backing tracks done, and some of the vocals before Jon got involved again.

JK: Were you surprised at the success of *90125* straight out of the box as it was? It did give you your first number-one single in America with "Owner of a Lonely Heart."

AW: Oh yeah. It was commercially the band's biggest album. I forget exactly how many millions that album sold, but it was quite a lot.

JK: I think despite what many say about the various members coming and going in and out of Yes, it has actually kept the band going, rather than being something detrimental. Whenever someone new comes in, or someone comes back, it seems to reignite the band and bring a new force and creativity with it.

AW: Well, that seems to be the thing that happens, and with new blood, I suppose that always makes people raise their game somewhat. It's what's happening now with the new singer, Jon Davison. The band's on fire, really.

JK: So that for you personally makes you think, *I have to up my game here*, when someone new comes in because you have been through several changes with Yes over the last 40 years.

AW: Yes, it does. You have to buck up and go, "Hey, this is really happening."

JK: What was it like when you recorded *Fly From Here*, and Geoff Downes came back into the band? For instance, how did you feel about bringing the song 'Fly From Here' back to the table and working on it?

AW: Well I remember well when we did the original version and played it live on the *Drama* tour, and particularly at Madison Square Gardens. But it was really more of a pop song then, to be honest. It was done in a very "Poppy" way, in fact very much like a Buggles way, which of course it would be, as Trevor and Geoff wrote it.

JK: It's much more a Yes song now though isn't it?

AW: Well, we changed it around a lot into a Yes song, where the rhythm section changes around all the time, and it fits in more with what we do as Yes. And that album has done really, really well, to be honest. It's been a bit of a sleeper like a lot of Yes albums, and it is nice that it has been so successful.

JK: It is the band's 45th anniversary in 2013. How do you feel approaching that milestone?

AW: I know that we have a tour booked in February that goes through March, and we are doing a special event in March [Cruise To The Edge], so we are all getting geared up for that now and brushing up on stuff we haven't played for quite a while. We are performing three whole albums in the set: *The Yes Album*, *Close To The Edge*, and *Going For The One*, so hopefully we will all be ready to play them! (*Laughs*) The feeling in the band is very good right now, I have to tell you.

JK: How did you decide on which three albums the band would be performing on the tour?

AW: (*Laughs*) Well that was a hell of a long process, I can tell you! There was a lot of discussion going back and forth. We batted around a number of albums for a long while before deciding on those three. There were all sorts of combinations and *Fragile* was going to be in there for a while, but there are so many albums to choose from, really. *Drama* was considered too. There is a whole different type of show you can do depending on which albums you choose to perform because of the different era changes.

JK: I suppose with Yes – because there are so many different eras and some fans like some eras more than others – it would be an impossible task to please everyone, so you just have to go with what you feel to be the best way forward and choose a set that you think will reach the biggest audience.

AW: Well you know, you can always count on *Close To The Edge* because that is a little bit of a stalwart album, and of course, a lot of people like it.

JK: I think many people consider that to be the definitive Yes album.

AW: Well as for the songs like "Close To The Edge", "And You And I", and "Siberian Khatru", these are songs that we have played for a very long time, no matter what the lineup or wherever we have played them in the world. Those songs are key songs in the Yes set. So yeah, *Close To The Edge* is important as an album, but in another light, *90125* is just as important but appeals to a different crowd. It's strange really, as it affects different generations, I suppose.

JK: I presume that this year will see another World tour then, including the UK?

AW: Well, I have to tell you, Jon, I always push for us to play in Liverpool when we play the UK. I get so many requests when I do the Beatles festival every summer – well, I try to do it every summer. I didn't do it this year, but it is such a great city, and the festival is such a great thing to do all week. But I do get asked all the time about Yes playing there, and we do very well in Liverpool, we always have done. But the band has done incredibly well live all over the world in the last year or so. It has been very satisfying, to be honest.

At the time of this interview, Alan was preparing for a special concert with an orchestra in his home of Seattle. But as he said, he would soon be getting to grips with rehearsals for the forthcoming tour where Yes would be performing three albums in their entirety – something that most Yes fans will be excited to see in a live situation. The band also headlines the Cruise To The Edge event in March 2013. As ever, the rumour mill is alive with gossip surrounding the other plans for Yes in their anniversary year, and as ever, Yes will surely rise to the occasion and bring their particular brand of magic to stages around the world.

2019 Update
Yes celebrated their 50th Anniversary in fine style in 2018, and a live album and film documenting the anniversary was released in the summer of 2019. Alan has also undergone back surgery, which means that he only plays a part of the live Yes set. During the rest of the concert, Jay Schellen plays with Yes. Jay has previously worked with Billy Sherwood, Geoff Downes, and Chris Squire. Alan is slowly recuperating and able to play more of the set as time moves on.

~

Geoff Downes: Drama
Switzerland, March 2002

In March 2002, I was lucky enough to be on tour with the then-current line-up of Asia. The band were touring Europe as part of a world tour to celebrate their 20th Anniversary. Geoff and I managed to find some time to talk about the *Drama* period of Yes, just after the soundcheck in Pratelln, Switzerland.

Jon Kirkman (JK): I am going back 22 years now, or maybe a little bit longer. A lot of people were surprised when the *Drama* album came out, but it wasn't because Yes had brought out another album. The big shock was that Rick Wakeman had left, and you had replaced him, and Jon Anderson had left, and Trevor Horn had joined. If that wasn't bad enough for the Yes fans, add the fact that you guys were known as the very successful pop group, the Buggles. How did it feel at the time?

Geoff Downes (GD): It was really strange when I think about it in hindsight, because Yes had always been this revered progressive rock band, and we were seen as coming in there as a couple of imposters, if you like. They saw us as a couple of pop guys coming in and joining "our band," so we got quite a lot of resentment from the die-hard Yes fans. They thought that we had somehow desecrated the Yes legacy. From our own standpoint, it didn't really seem that weird. There was a lot of press about it, and they called us the Yeggles and things like that. It was very tongue in cheek. But as far as the album was concerned, when people took it at face value, it was a good album. I think that whether you are a Yes purist or not, the fact is the previous album, *Tormato*, had not been a popular album with the Yes fans. The *Drama* album stood up as being a step in the right direction for Yes, at that point. It wasn't as hard for me as it was for Trevor. Trevor had the unenviable task of taking over from Yes' only lead singer, whereas Yes had had three previous keyboard players, so it wasn't so bad for me.

JK: Do you think in hindsight that a lot of Yes fans have come to regard that album quite highly? Without wishing to knock some of the other Yes albums, it has stood the test of time very well, hasn't it?

GD: I think it has. Tracks like "Machine Messiah" and "Tempus Fugit" were very much Yes tracks. I think that once we had got over the fact that we had decided to go ahead with the merger, although we did some stuff with the Buggles later in the year, it virtually killed that concept. Having joined Yes at that point, we just got our heads down and got on with the album. A lot of work went into the album, and I think it is a good album. There was no disgrace in that album.

JK: If we go back a little earlier than that, the main approach came from Chris Squire, but you did actually share management, didn't you? Brian Lane was managing the Buggles and Yes at that time, wasn't he?

GD: I think it was actually a culmination of a number of factors. The fact was, Trevor was a singer, and I was the keyboard player, and that was our little entity. Yes were working just as a three-piece, without a singer and keyboard player, because Anderson and Wakeman had gone at that time. We were both managed by Brian Lane, and he was, in some way, instrumental in suggesting it. The actual initial thing came about when Brian Lane asked us to write a track for Yes, who were then rehearsing as a three-piece at the Town House studios with Chris, Alan, and Steve. We wrote a song that was called, "You Can Fly From Here," which a few people will have on bootlegs and that sort of thing. We did it with Bill Bruford and Chris Squire, and that was one of the tracks that was actually put forward on *Drama*. We actually did record it, and then the other material came about. We had "I Am A Camera," which was then modified into Yes fashion and became a much longer track called "Into The Lens," but effectively it was the same song. Trevor and I had the bones for that song. We went into a few rehearsals and came up for a few bits for "Machine Messiah," and then Brian suggested we should go with it and do a Yes album. We had to see Ahmet Ertegun, who was the head of Atlantic records then. He came over and had a listen and said, "Yes, go with it." That was pretty much the background of how it came about. Chris wanted to bring Eddie Offord into the frame because they had classic Yes albums done by Offord. I think it was that era, more than anything else, that we were allied to, rather than the *Relayer* or *Going For The One* period. Chris Squire wanted to go back more to the field of *The Yes Album* and *Fragile*, and if you look at the setlist, we did much of that material at the time.

JK: I think a lot of the material on *Drama* compares quite favourably with *The Yes Album* and *Fragile*, certainly the keyboard sound. Was that deliberate?

GD: I had been a big Yes fan when I was at school, so there was a bit of an age difference there. I mean, not a lot, because they were going when they were in their early 20s, but I was just doing my A levels, and I was listening to *Time And A Word* and things like that. I was really into some of the basic orchestrations that Tony Kaye was doing on that stuff. I suppose my role in the situation was a mix of the type of keyboard playing on *The Yes Album* and the stuff on *Fragile* that was a bit more virtuoso. That was the kind of player that I was – a blend of those two types of players, and that was what worked very well towards the "Machine Messiah" concept of the keyboards on *Drama*.

JK: Having recorded *Drama*, Yes were presumably expected to tour that album. Trevor Horn had said to Chris Squire at the time, "You do realise that I am going to have to sing this in front of a lot of people, probably at Madison Square Garden, and I don't know whether I can." It was Chris Squire that talked him into it and told him that he could. There must have been a heck of a lot of nerves in the Yes camp when the band went out with that line-up and that album, despite however strong you felt that the album may have been.

GD: Yeah, I think people were concerned, like Phil Carson at Atlantic – he was their point person in the UK. I think there was a lot of worry because the tour had already been booked. The American tour had already been put in, you know, three nights in Madison Square Garden, a couple of nights at Philadelphia Spectrum…you are talking about a seriously big package. And the thing was not whether I could cut it particularly, but whether Trevor could cut the vocals that Jon Anderson had made so personal to himself. Someone like Jon Anderson has a very individual and very recognisable voice, not only in the range of high proximity of the register but his general projection of the lyrics and that sort of thing. That was what concerned Trevor more than anything else. It was largely Chris that said, "No, you can do it, you can do it." It got to the point where we had to do it. That was it, the tour was booked, and we were on the plane. We were rehearsed, and that was it.

JK: Performing *Drama* live must have been a little difficult for Trevor. On the studio album, it is not too bad, he is not unlike Jon Anderson, but he wasn't really "road-tested," if you like, as a singer and a lot of people do not realise how much it takes it out of a singer, do they?

GD: No, it is very hard. I have worked with a lot of great singers – John Wetton, Greg Lake, John Payne, Glen Hughes – people I would consider to the at the top end of the progressive rock singing area. And the stuff that I had done with Trevor before Yes, he was very much a chameleon type of vocalist. He was good at imitating people. A lot of the Buggles concept was based around the gimmickry we put on his voice. I think what happened in the Yes thing was that he almost had to learn to sing like Jon Anderson, and that is not easy. At times he carried it off, and at others, he didn't. A lot of the stuff was very high, and Chris and Steve did not want to transpose anything down. "And You And I" is way up there!

JK: "And You And I" is a case in point. I spoke to Chris Squire about this once. He said that Trevor's problem was that he wasn't consistent enough on the road, but in the studio he was fine. There was one particular incident in Texas, and he told Trevor when they came off stage that he had sung "And You And I" better than Jon Anderson. But unfortunately, he wasn't able to maintain that consistency throughout the tour.

GD: I think that is the classic thing. Trevor himself never considered himself to be a vocalist, by any stretch of the imagination. He was a bass player; that was where Trevor came from. When I started working with him on the Buggles, he was a session bass player, which was his job. He had a little thing about having a small recording studio that he used to tinker around and experiment with. Vocals were not his bag. Bearing in mind what we had to pull off, for the most part, came across okay. It wasn't so bad in America; I think it was when we got into England. When we were in Madison Square Garden, we were so far away from the audience the whole thing became like a pageant almost. The critical ear is not so heavily levelled because you have got the event value. When we came to the UK, we had this quite extensive theatre tour booked. We were right in front of the audience, and that was when there was quite a bit of barracking coming in, particularly aimed at Trevor. In the defunct Sounds magazine, someone said it was like having Ronnie Corbett up there or something like that.

JK: I actually saw you on two occasions on that tour. I saw you at Deeside, which was quite good, but in Manchester, I think some people just paid to go and hurl abuse. That's the English thing, I know. They're a lot more open in Europe and in the UK, and with you saying it was almost Jon Anderson's band, how dare this interloper come in? In Manchester, I was quite surprised because it was vitriolic at times throughout the set.

GD: Yeah, any time there was a quiet moment... And in Yes' music, there are some poignant moments when there is not a lot going on, and then it builds up again, and in those moments you would hear someone yelling out, "Get off," or "Bring back Anderson," and all this sort of thing. Fair play to Trevor, he could obviously hear it. I think it put him off, and I think he thought that he was just going to be a producer now – "I don't need this grief!" I think that is pretty much what set him on that route as an exclusive thing. He was never very happy being an artist; it was never something that came to him naturally. Even in the Buggles thing, he didn't like the limelight that it threw on him. He wasn't comfortable in that role; whereas I was happy in that role, being the artist. I was happy doing all the pieces of promotion that you had to do. I was quite happy to go out on the stage. Just going back to that first moment in Toronto's Maple Leaf Gardens, I was hooked. We played to

18,000 people that night, and that was the very first time that I had played to anywhere near that number of people. That was a magic moment.

JK: When you and Trevor went into Yes, you must have thought, *Let's see a little further down the road; let's see how this goes with the album and the tour.* When did it become apparent that that particular line-up wasn't going to go any further than the one album and the one world tour? Would have been the UK dates?

GD: I think it was the London dates. We sort of got around the rest of the UK. As you say, we did Deeside Leisure centre, Manchester, and did three great nights at Glasgow Apollo and Newcastle City Hall. And they were all good! It was when we went down south where people were a little bit more cynical, particularly the London crowd. We had three nights at the Hammersmith Odeon, as it was then, and two nights at Finsbury Park. I think it was the Finsbury Park (The Rainbow Theatre) gigs that did it because we were very close to the audience and you could see a real animosity coming from the audience towards what we were doing. I think at this point, Chris was starting to doubt the wisdom of what he had orchestrated by getting Trevor and I involved in it. From that point, it was clear that nothing else was going to happen after that final gig, either at Hammersmith Odeon or Finsbury Park. Everyone went home that night thinking, *No, this is just not going to happen.*

JK: I have spoken to a lot of the guys in Yes over the years, and Rick Wakeman has been very honest and said that at the time he dismissed it and that it wasn't a Yes album. But in hindsight, he thinks that *Drama* is a very important album. Without *Drama*, Yes might not be going today. There couldn't have been *90125*, and that was a very transitional album. Would you agree?

GD: Well, yeah. I remember Rick Wakeman saying things at the time. He was very dismissive in a couple of radio interviews of the whole Yes thing at that point, saying that without him and Jon, how could they call it Yes? If that is the thinking that he has latterly come to, he is right in terms of the fact that *Drama* bridged the gap between what was considered to be the old Yes and the new Yes, which was Trevor Rabin and the *90125* version. *Drama* sort of sits right bang in the middle as a transitionary album that took Yes into a new generation. The Yes of *90125* is a very different Yes to the one of *Tormato*, and *Drama* fits in the middle there.

JK: At the end of the *Drama* tour, we have read that Yes boiled down basically to yourself and Steve Howe. Trevor did not want to be involved, obviously, and Alan and Chris had gone off to work with Jimmy Page and possibly

Robert Plant. Was there ever a consideration to continue Yes with just you two, or was it a case of, "Let's just go and start another band," which became Asia, obviously.

GD: Well, I talked to Steve about it shortly after. Of all of them, Steve and I had a very good understanding. I know that he liked my style of keyboard playing, which I think he felt it very much complimented his style of guitar playing. It is quite a difficult blend to get in a group, where, at times you have them covering the same territory and have to get them to work together. We actually did build up quite a good rapport. When Chris and Alan had started going off as XYZ (as it was called then tentatively) and were rehearsing with Jimmy Page, I had had a few conversations with Steve. He was sort of talking about him and me picking up the reins of Yes and getting some extra players in; that kind of thing. It was sort of left in abeyance. He was waiting to see what happened with the other side at that point, which was Chris, Alan, and Jimmy Page. Also, at that time, I was working with Trevor. He had said he was out of this Yes thing now, and we were contracted to do another Buggles album with Island, so we started getting on with that in January.

I think it was December 1980 when we did the last gigs, and in January we started doing some demos for the second Buggles album, *Adventures In Modern Recording*. It was really during those demos, I think, that Steve gave me a call and told me he had started to work with John Wetton, and there was the talk of a new band being put together. He asked if I would be interested, so I said, "Yeah, definitely!" He said that it would be a completely new thing and there was a possibility that Geffen Records might show an interest in putting something together for a band made up of John Wetton, himself, plus me. They said that they were going to audition a few drummers, so I went along, and we did a rehearsal with, funnily enough, Simon Phillips. This was in February 1981. We went to see Simon Philips, who was playing with Jeff Beck at the time, at Hammersmith. Simon came down for a couple of days and rehearsed with Steve, John Wetton, and myself. I was starting to get few calls from John Wetton as well because he said that he would really like to work me on some things. We started to build up a bit of a friendship there, and this was how the whole thing kind of snowballed. Then I went back to do some more stuff with Trevor on the Buggles thing. At that time, they contacted Carl Palmer because Simon Phillips wasn't interested in doing it, or was too busy, or whatever. They were working with Carl Palmer and asked if I wanted to come down to the rehearsals and have a go with the four of them. That was it, really. I told Trevor that I had this opportunity to do this band with Steve Howe, John Wetton, and Carl Palmer and that I would like to take it because that's the way it is.

JK: Of course, this year sees the 20th Anniversary of Asia. Now, a lot of rumours tend to come from the internet, which is not the most reliable of sources. Yes went through the *Union* phase and there was a big version of Yes doing the rounds. They made an album called *Union*, and the current rumour is that there is going to be another one of those, but with everybody who has been involved in Yes doing maybe an album and a tour. If schedules allow (and I know that Asia are very, very busy with touring next year, and possibly some more recording), but if the schedules could be matched up, would you be interested in doing something like that?

GD: I am always in two minds. Over the years, I have had occasional calls from Yes to see if I would go back and do tours with them, and it has either not fitted in with my schedule, or they have re-thought the situation. Over the last seven or eight years, I have had various calls from time to time, and as I say, I am in two minds about it. A complete tour comprising every single member of Yes, I am not sure that it would work, to be honest. I am not pouring cold water on that, but I just remember the *Union* tour, and people said that two drummers on stage is a hell of a lot to take in. It is a hell of a lot of information to have two guitarists.

JK: I think the plan this time around might be a big profile show at somewhere like the Royal Albert Hall, and a Yes through the ages type thing. In other words, starting off with the original band, and then other members coming on stage and working like that.

GD: Something like that might be an interesting one-off, but in terms of mileage, I don't see where it would go. I think it would be a nice historical statement, and you could maybe do an album of that concert or something like that. That sort of thing might be good, whether or not you would get everyone though… I would probably do it if I didn't have anything else to do that night and Asia weren't touring, but to me, Asia comes first. It comes first and foremost above everything. But if it was possible, I would do it. John Wetton has just asked me to play on his one-off convention that he is doing, which I may well do. There is no harm in doing those things; you can't turn around and forsake your roots. There are a lot more difficult people than me involved in the whole Yes legacy thing, I can tell you!

JK: Twenty-two years down the road, the *Drama* period is probably still one of the most contentious periods in Yes' history. Presumably, though, you must have quite happy memories of that year. There was a lot in that year, wasn't there?

GD: There was a lot in that year because even when we joined, there was still a lot of Buggles fever around in Europe. The record was breaking in Europe a lot later than it was here, and that whole period from about September 1979 to September 1980 had an enormous amount of things happen for me. The Buggles thing came out and went to number-one, six months later we were doing a Yes album and six months after that we were playing Madison Square Gardens in Yes. We had done two albums in that time, so it was a very intense period of time, in terms of record promotion and the whole rest of it. As far as Yes goes, the album *Drama* was called *Drama* for a very good reason. There were probably three or four episodes of Spinal Tap in that one *Drama* album in the making. Eddie Offord came, flipped out, and went. I can remember most of it pretty clearly, and I remember thinking that it was absolutely nuts, this is really crazy.

JK: Having said that, it is still an excellent album.

GD: A lot of people really like tracks like "Tempus Fugit" and "Machine Messiah." I am surprised that even Jon Anderson wouldn't get off on singing something that he did not have a creative role in himself. If Yes did get out there and they did do "Machine Messiah," or they did "Tempus Fugit," I think it would go down well, but who knows?

JK: Cheers, Geoff!

GD: Thank you.

Following the European leg of the tour, Asia toured America and recorded another studio album before Geoff reunited with the original line-up of Asia in 2006 and celebrated the band's 25th Anniversary. More importantly, in November 2004, Geoff played with a version of Yes that included Trevor Horn, Steve Howe, Alan White, Chris Squire, and Steve Howe for a concert to celebrate Trevor Horn's career in music. The concert was a one-off for the Princes Trust; however in early 2011, it was announced that Geoff Downes was returning to Yes to record the band's new album *Fly From Here*. The album was produced by Trevor Horn, so at least in the studio, this saw the reunion of the *Drama* line-up.

∼

Jon Anderson: The More You Know
Liverpool, April 1998

In March 1998, Yes embarked on what was their first UK tour in over seven years. The band were promoting their latest album, *Open Your Eyes*. The tour was sold out, and while promoting the album, Jon Anderson also wanted to promote his latest solo album, *The More You Know*. It was in a hotel after the Yes concert that I spoke to Jon.

Jon Kirkman (JK): You have a solo album out at the moment: *The More You Know*. You mentioned earlier that you have had some albums out that have not been available in this country. I have actually seen them on import. You always seem very eclectic in your choice of albums, but the new album is very pop-orientated.

Jon Anderson (JA): Yeah it is a sort of world music, R&B, jazz sort of thing. I really love it. I think it should sell ten million! (*Laughs*) I don't know if that will happen. I had a dream that it was going to be a big record and I was going to be like Phil Collins – a big megastar.

JK: It is the sort of album that, if it is picked up by radio in America and in this country, it has some very commercial tracks on it. Your earlier albums, *Olias*, of course, and then there was *Song of Seven*, was also a commercial-sounding album. Do you ever think that, *if this does not work, I am going to carry on doing these things anyway*?

JA: Why not? I know that my next album is going to be Arabic music. I am very interested in travelling the world and making music, so I would love to do this Arabic-style of music. And my friend Francis [Jocky], who did *The More You Know* with me, has been spending time in Egypt these last couple of months, and he has been doing some recording. Then I have an idea that I want to do an album for the Millennium, a special album that I have been writing for about three years, so I will probably do that as well. I will probably put an album out every month and see if one hits. It's like going to Las Vegas. Maybe I don't want to be famous in that sense, you know, like a megastar. Maybe I like making music so much that eventually people who like music will understand this life that I have gone through musically, and enjoy what I did. Eventually, when I am about a hundred and three, they will say, "He was pretty good!"

JK: Do you sometimes prefer the albums you make for yourself, rather than the ones you know the record companies will like?

JA: Actually, I have only done two albums for the record company, and it didn't work anyway so… One was *Song of Seven*. I was trying to make an album that was commercial. I had just left Yes, and it wasn't commercial at all. Then I tried to do an album called *In The City Of Angels*, and if Phil had sung those songs, they would have been hits. They were good songs. In fact, the song I put out as a single was with Lamont Dozier, and then Phil worked with him a couple of months later, and he had a hit record. And I thought, *My God, I think I am two months behind!*

JK: As opposed to being ahead, as sometimes people say you are with Yes.

JA: Yeah. I have this strange sort of belief system that I am sort of not ready yet for mega-stardom.

JK: Do you think you will do any live solo gigs? I have seen some footage around about the time of *Toltec*, when you were playing with South American musicians I saw you do a version of "Owner Of A Lonely Heart," which was very interesting.

JA: It was an acoustic version, because in "Owner Of A Lonely Heart," the chords are "Twist And Shout." I sang it tonight. You didn't hear me sing it, did you?

JK: I didn't, to be honest with you, no.

JA: I got to the end of "Owner Of A Lonely Heart," and I said, "Shake it up baby, twist and shout, come on, come on" right at the very end, and it went into the guitar solo. Yeah, it is the same chords as "Twist and Shout" and "La Bamba". When I went on this South American tour, I used to jiggle them up and do a bit of each song. It was very acoustic. I am very fortunate; 35 years ago, I was in the Cavern doing dinner time sessions, and here I am travelling around the world, sometimes doing exactly what I want to do. I can go to Peru or Indonesia, and people will say, "You're that guy, Jon Van Gellis" or, "You're Yes, aren't you?" Life is a wonderful experience, and I'm very lucky to still be making music and still enjoy singing, as you heard tonight.

JK: It was a great gig tonight. I have to be honest, I would like to see some solo Jon Anderson gigs. But more importantly, you can't leave it 24 years before you come and play in Liverpool again, because tonight's gig was incredible!

JA: Well, all I have to say to finish off this wonderful conversation is, I need a good manager!

JK: (*Laughs*) And if he hears this, he will probably kill you! Jon, it has been an absolute pleasure talking to you this evening. Thanks for having a chat with us. Keep doing what you are doing. I really like your solo album; it is absolutely wonderful! We have been playing it a lot on Rockahead, and we look forward to hearing not just solo albums, but also Yes albums from Jon Anderson.

JA: Thanks a lot! You take care now.

And with that, Jon was back to the bar for more Guinness. He brought us all back some drinks while Alan, Chris, Igor, and I discussed the French film that was playing on the television. While in the bar, we were all amused by comments and jokes from Jon, who proved that if he ever decided to get tired of singing, he certainly has a career ahead of him as a comedian. Perhaps he has taken tips from Rick Wakeman. Jon was to continue with Yes for another six years before leaving the band in early 2004. His solo career, however, continues unabated.

∼

Steve Howe: An Opportunity
September 2012

Steve Howe had previously worked up a reputation as guitarist with British psychedelic band Tomorrow, who enjoyed a hit with their song "My White Bicycle." Following Tomorrow, Steve joined the band Bodast, a band who recorded one album that was unreleased at the time. When Steve joined Yes in the summer of 1970 following the departure of Peter Banks, the band were on the verge of releasing their second studio album. Record company executives in America thought the original cover for *Time And A Word* was too risqué, which necessitated another cover. A shot of the band was substituted for the American release, while the UK and European release retained the original design. However, there was a problem; the band picture used for the sleeve included Steve Howe, who wasn't actually on the album. It must be said that neither Steve nor Peter were particularly happy about this at the time, but Steve did fit into the band very well, and in the next two years, the band managed to record three hugely successful albums and break America.

Jon Kirkman (JK): I have been looking at some of the statistics. Between you joining in 1970 and the summer of 1972, there were three albums, almost 300 live dates, and Yes got a new manager, Eddie Offord, who came into the picture as co-producer. There just seems to have been so much happening at the time.

Steve Howe (SH): Well, it all spawned from *The Yes Album* itself, really. We didn't use Roger [Dean] on that; we used him on the *Fragile* album. As we got organised to do *The Yes Album*, as you said, a new manager came on board. Then it seemed to accelerate. We didn't notice it. To make *Fragile* and *Close To The Edge* – both of which are very quintessential records by Yes – in the same period was astounding. That does cover the period you are interested in.

JK: Were you actually aware of Yes before you were approached to join the band?

SH: Well, I was aware of them, but I didn't quite understand them, or really had an idea that I had ever really heard them, but I had heard of their reputation.

JK: Do you think it is fair to say that even though the first two albums were very good albums of their time, it was when you recorded *The Yes Album* that everything really came together?

SH: Well, my feeling when I joined the band was that I was not keen on being in a band that played other people's material. I had spent that little bit of time in between Tomorrow and being in Yes in a band called Bodast. And the sentiment there was that we played what we wrote, and so the quality would show. The recordings are only as good as the songs. That was a challenge that I wanted to see Yes do. So, I encouraged them to do an album of their own material because they had already done two with lots of covers on them. They were very good covers, and Bill helped a lot in making the arrangements for things like "Everydays" and all the other songs, and like the arrangements we did later for "America" by Paul Simon. This was all done in around the same period we are talking about.

JK: When you joined the band, it seemed to me that the first thing you had to do was to promote the previous album. It came out just after you joined, didn't it?

SH: Yes, it was a bad piece of timing, really. They invited me when *Time And A Word* was just coming out, hence the photograph that Barry Wentzell took of us in Wardour Street in his studio. It ended up on the cover because America rejected the sexist picture on *Time And A Word*, but accepted a picture with me in it. I got very cross with Atlantic years later, saying, "Stop doing this!" I was telling them that they can't keep putting my picture on *Time And A Word*.

JK: How difficult was it for you coming into the band and having to perform older material? Presumably, you wanted to put your own spin on it.

SH: Yeah, I did. I have never found it easy copying other guitarists, even someone I really like such as Wes Montgomery or Chet Atkins. To copy them was almost a crime, so when I was asked to copy things by Peter Banks, I could only take them so far. In retrospect, some of the things I did do with the songs are actually quite good. I have heard some early recordings of us playing "Astral Traveller" and other songs, where I was having quite a bit of fun. So I was quite capable of playing these arrangements and tweaking where I couldn't learn or wasn't going to be bothered, or was unable to play every note that Peter Banks played, or didn't want to. I really liked what he played, and really, he did set the scene for me very well, because he was quite an original guitarist and he did colour it with different styles, which is obviously what I did, even more.

JK: You did some live gigs, and then the decision was made that a new album was needed. The band did what a lot of bands did, and went away to a farm in Devon, which is about getting away to the country to get it together, as they said in the 60s. How much time was spent in Devon putting *The Yes Album* together?

SH: We spent two weeks in a little town called Churchwood, just north of Barnstaple. We didn't like it there. We couldn't make enough noise at night, and it was all very restricted. It was like a kind of bed and breakfast place. The promoter down there, whose name I think was Mike, advertised in the local paper: "Rock Group Looking For Somewhere To Rehearse In North Devon." We found the perfect spot, and we were there for two months in South Molton. My wife and I now own that house because we fell in love with it then. We didn't buy it then. What happened there was like something I hadn't imagined, but enjoyed so much because I had spent my childhood in London, and that was where everybody wanted to come. Strangely enough, when I went to Devon, I decided I wanted to go there. I think the music really benefitted from that experience, which was a kind of cliché in itself. Spooky Tooth went out to Reading, and other groups were starting to head for the country for this focus and peace and quiet. Having said that, *Fragile* was mostly composed in London, as was *Close To The Edge*, but based on the music we had written while we were on tour, mainly. Jon and I collaborated, and it became quite a song-writing strength at that time. There was just the embryo of an album when we collaborated on things like "Starship Trooper" and "Yours Is No Disgrace." I was finding my feet. The best thing they ever said to me when I had written this instrumental called "Clap," which was just for guitar, was that I should stick it on the album. So, I thought, *Right! I'm sticking this on the album!* That was an opportunity I couldn't miss! All of those things combined to make a style of Yes music that hadn't quite been yet. As we were saying, when they did the cover material, it was brilliantly arranged; it was just spectacular. But when we did our own material, we applied the same arrangement skills.

JK: So, when the album came together, did you have nearly all the material there? I think you brought "Wurm" to the sessions, which was a hangover from the Bodast days?

SH: Yeah, it was a song called "The Ghost Of Nether Street," which was a street in Finchley that we lived in, and I had those lines, and the melody, and the three chords, and Yes liked that. So there was a sense, as I said, of collaboration, as I've pointed out right from the word go. There was a feeling of respect amongst us that created the chemistry and meant that we could do really good things together.

JK: Was your first gig the live recording of "Clap" at the Lyceum?

SH: No, it wasn't. People seem to think it was, but I did some other gigs. I can't really remember where they were. I think somebody has got the right date, but there were other gigs before the Lyceum. That was a bit of a mad thing to do, for some reason we did it that way. We may have tried it in the studio. I wanted to say, *The Yes Album* wasn't made like records were in the 80s and 90s, when you just took out a whole period and said, "We are going to make a record." We made *The Yes Album* and *Fragile* while out on tour, in between little bits of touring. We would go back in, do a few days, and fix up a song. That meant that the material on the album kind of grew as we took it out on stage and tried to play it. When I first toured, we only had the embryo of some of the songs off *The Yes Album* and *Time And A Word* to play.

JK: The studio version of "Clap" is actually on the re-mastered version of *The Yes Album*. It is a great piece of music. You must be very proud of that because you still play that live today.

SH: Yeah, do you mean as a bonus track? There is a portion when I play "Mood For A Day" and "Clap." I think that was recorded after I did the live version. There were a few mix-ups on those box sets when they wouldn't listen to me. I was brought in as a guiding light on finding stuff, and I had 60 tapes, which they took away. But without over-expanding on that story, all I wanted was to change what it said on that reissue, what Jon says just before I play it, because he generally said, "Steve is going to play a tune called 'Clap'," but that night he said that I was going to play a song called "The Clap," and that labelled the song with a new title that had nothing to do with why it was called "Clap" – it was a clap along. I have recorded the other version a couple of times on live albums, and also a studio version of that on an album called *Motif*, which was on electric guitar. So I do secretively know many of the ingredients that pushed me to write that piece, but the fact that I finished it on the night Dylan was born was an amazing thing. Not a fluke, but an amazing thing to couple with it. I was so excited by it, but really it was a huge tribute to my love of Chet Atkins and his style of playing.

JK: You said that *The Yes Album* was recorded in between tour dates, and I've looked at some of the archives notes of some of the albums. There did seem to be a number of sessions for the album. I know that when bands go in to record if they are touring, they sometimes, as you said, try songs out live and that sometimes changes the feel and the arrangement. How much of the material changed during these sessions? Was there much of that with *The Yes Album*?

SH: More! I would say that was a pattern that we adopted all the way through the 70s. We would get a song to a certain point in the rehearsal room and then put it on a cassette, and then later on a Revox quarter-inch tape machine so that we would have a version or bits of it. Then we would just make it about a hundred per cent better. We would streamline it, cut this and that, and get the track down. Very often, not underestimating Rick's incredible contribution to *Fragile* and *Close To The Edge*, but he wasn't there as much as we were. We were working on the album, and Rick flitted in and did more overdub parts. That enabled Chris, Bill, and myself to work very closely with Eddie, and Jon of course, to get these backing tracks down. It was very, very exciting. That is when things started to take shape, and they started to sound much better. I didn't want a group that had too much drumming or guitar, and if anytime that went on, we would come up with parts or riffs; better ideas to improve the songs. So, yeah, the construction was already something that we all cared a lot about at that time. We did it in a very old-fashioned way, where we just kept doing it in a rehearsal room. But when we went into the studio, it really did take on another life altogether, and became properly "studio-ised" and properly produced.

JK: How important was Eddie Offord to the Yes mix? He had previously been the engineer on *Time And A Word*, he had got the co-producers credit starting with *The Yes Album*, and I think the last album he did in the 70s was *Relayer*. Then he came back briefly with *Drama*. So just how important was Eddie, because he also did the live sound as well, didn't he?

SH: Well, there is a sort of mixed answer about that one because his importance on the record was enormous, and we shared that production credit with him with great justification. It was all done very naturally; in other words, he didn't feel he was set up for the job, so he didn't feel under pressure. He had the honesty and truth about him to say if something wasn't good enough, try another one, or it was better three times before. He had good ears, and great skills at engineering and editing, and the flamboyance kind of came later. At first, he was almost like a boffin sort of guy who worked on the engineering. Along the way, his skills helped to make us famous, and the tight little sound that we had with jazzy drums and my very clean guitar compared to the bluesy sound with finger vibratos. We all brought a different creature to the table, but Eddie knew best how to get that mix. But we all mixed the albums, in those early days. We all sat there with the exclusion of Rick (I don't know if occasionally other exclusions happened), but we would all grab faders, and usually, Eddie would do the drums, Jon would look at the vocals, Chris would be thumping the bass, and I would be thumping the guitar. We would do that as a team, so Eddie's role was great. We went on tour, and at the time it was spectacular what it did for us on the road. But then it became patchy and problematic; a bit too out there, a bit too spaced out, and we were more used to being on the road than Eddie was, so it all became a bit too much for Eddie.

He became a star in his own right, which was justifiable, but he became a liability that we couldn't use, so we had to part company around the time we did *Going For The One*. When he came back for *Drama* that was only a very fleeting period. He actually didn't complete all of the backing tracks. It is credited that Eddie did them, but we also had Hugh Padgham, Trevor Horn, – we had our own production concepts – and Gary Langan helped to mix the albums. So there was a lot of teamwork on that record, and it wasn't much about Eddie, as he only did the first couple of weeks on it and then we got to grips with it ourselves.

JK: When you went to America for the very first time, were you surprised at how well Yes were appreciated and how well the audience took to them? Yes weren't really your typical American touring band. You had to sit and listen to Yes; they weren't a boogie band.

SH: You are absolutely right. Jethro Tull was the first band we toured with, and we always give them the tribute that they gave us the opportunity to play. The first gig was actually in Canada. We opened for them in Edmonton, and from that very first night, I knew that we were going to make a wave here. What happened was, there were about 15,000 people in a huge Jethro Tull event/gig, and we went on first, and they just loved us! They really, really loved us. We could tell, we could feel that there was a connection, but we wondered if it was because it was Canada. But the same thing happened when we went to America. For some reason, our song and the little bit of exposure we had meant that Yes was really quite exciting, right from the word "Go," so it is not surprising that we very quickly became a headliner and didn't open for anybody. It was fantastic to feel the pleasure we're giving the audiences. It had already happened with Jethro Tull, and suddenly they liked Yes, so that was a great sign, and that filled me with enthusiasm. I remember the half an hour before that first show just thinking, and I don't usually get nervous, but this was pretty exciting. A few things happened, we walked on stage, and it was like BANG! This is what we are meant for! Whatever we could achieve in Britain, we would love and hold very dear to our hearts, but success at that particular time meant charting in America; there was no doubt about that. We had gone there to pick up the ticket, to get famous internationally, you know, so that worked.

JK: How did you feel when the American label took a song like "Roundabout," for instance, and edited it down to a single?

SH: Well, we resented it somewhat because there had been long songs that had been hits like "McArthur Park," so we felt that "Roundabout" could have been a hit like it was, but their wisdom was actually right because, at the time, the radio may not have played such a long song from an unknown English band. But they did play "Roundabout," and it charted and got to become number something, I don't know if it was one, but it was high and so was *Fragile*. So this hoisted us to the level that we liked to think that we had already become accustomed to, which was quite a lot of success.

JK: How quickly then, did Yes become a headline act in America?

SH: I believe on the second tour, which was 1972. *Fragile* was doing so well. I think we split it a bit and did some openings and then started to do our own shows. We were very popular in what you might call a gymnasium on the college circuit with university students and got them behind us. In Ohio, they went crazy on us immediately, and then Pennsylvania did the same thing. Since then, Philadelphia has even had a Yes Day…it really has! I can't remember when it is, June or July, I think. That is just because we were so popular in Philadelphia.

JK: One thing I have always wanted to ask you: *The Yes Album* was the first big hit album in the UK. When you were coming in to do *Fragile* with a new keyboard player, was there any pressure on the band to be a further big success? Did the record company put any extra pressure on you?

SH: They were quite pleased with how well *The Yes Album* had done in the UK, so we did gain a lot of credibility there. But in America, *The Yes Album* got to 30, which meant that it surfaced, but it didn't penetrate. So they may have put pressure on. All I know is, we were over there with *Fragile*, and we met the guys at Atlantic. I'm not sure if it was Ahmet Ertegun. I got quite friendly with Ahmet Ertegun over the years and had a lot of respect for him, but we went in and said that we wanted them to push this one harder than they had *The Yes Album*. When they saw "Roundabout," they saw something that they could really use. I guess we did feel we had to push them, but they did quickly realise that we were on to something, and particularly Ahmet Ertegun. He became a great supporter of Yes and Led Zeppelin, and all of the other bands that he had.

JK: The next album, *Close To The Edge* is considered by many fans to be "THE" Yes album, and that was the album for me. I was 13 going on 14, and I came to the band via The Old Grey Whistle Test and the live concert they did with you. The first song by the band that really hit me was "And You and I", and I worked my way back after that. How did you feel about doing an album with just three tracks on it? That was pretty radical, even for 1972.

SH: Well, we were feeling very adventurous, very confident, and very determined that we could not compromise our music. We weren't going to say
that we had to do something because they wanted it. We were completely
uncompromising, and Jon and I wrote *Close To The Edge.* We presented, collaborated, and brought *Close To The Edge* to the band with the idea that this
would be a great huge piece of music, bigger than "Yours Is No Disgrace,"
which I think, at the time, was our longest piece at about 8 minutes long.
We told them that this was much bigger and was going to be huge. "And You
And I" is a great song as well although shorter, and a lot of arrangement time
went into actually playing that piece as it stands.

Similarly with "Siberian Khatru," these were intricate pieces that we just kind
of threw off, this was our style, this was what we did, these were the things
we played. We didn't have anybody saying, "Oh God, you have to make it
easier." What Eddie was doing – going back to him for a moment – was
meshing all of these things together: a complicated bass part, a keyboard
part, a guitar part, three vocals, and the drums. So, he was finding places for
all of these things to go. We were really lucky to have people who could cope
with us and our demands. We were leading edge. We were going to have the
best sound and the best lighting, just because we wanted them and it went
with the music. We had these very high goals and were very hard to please!

JK: Roy Clare actually built you a PA because he was so enamoured by the
sound of the band, wasn't he?

SH: We started using Roy Clare on that very first tour with Jethro Tull by
chance, but then we realised that these people were the best in America. At
the time, Roy was helping to design something that was later called Roy Box-
es, I think. We were in a kind of transition where the old PA we had bought
in England from Iron Butterfly for £5000 was a three-way system with cross
overs, and this was superior to anything WEM or Marshall had as a PA.
We had the best PA in England at that time. It was only suitable for smaller
venues, but I guess we used it at the Royal Albert Hall as well. It had RCA
Mixers just like a Joe Meek studio and big bins – W bins. When we went to
America, it had all been stylised and reinvented with W bins lying under the
stage, and the horns flew in the air, and you had mid-range. Roy decided that
this was too much to have.

So, Roy was getting inventive, and he has always said that this was a major
opportunity for him to work with Yes. And because of our clout and our
style, it was good to say Yes used Clare. As much as we said that, he kept

delivering all of this stuff. He bent over backwards for us. We still love Roy very much, and the same with Michael Tait, who went from being an all-around tech. He went to America. He's Australian actually, and he created Tait Towers, which is one of the most successful stage and lighting systems in the world. Take Roger Dean – we had one of the best artists in the world for doing this kind of work in the mood of Yes and in the mood of the prog movement. So, with those three, Roy Clare, Mike Tait, and Roger Dean, they were near geniuses we had working for us. Yet we took it for granted; they were our people, you know. We were very lucky with people like Eddie as well, and I guess the manager, whose name we keep on not mentioning! (*Laughs*) He also pulled his finger out quite a bit for us.

JK: It does seem that around that time, your concerts were more like events than concerts. There was lighting and staging and incredible music. It was more the realm of the classical music genre than rock, really.

SH: Well, we originally went on stage to the music from *2001: A Space Odyssey*, until we discovered that Grand Funk Railroad were doing that in America, so we looked for other pieces of music. Then we used the Firebird suite for pretty much most of our career. That showed we were thinking classical, as you say. That kind of richness of sound, and not just a beat and a rhythm and a song. We had aspirations, and we tried to make them work on mellotrons. So, as you say, the concert was turning into a show, and the transition for that was really the next album, *Tales From Topographic Oceans*. That was when Roger Dean's staging first happened; we had the pods with lights in them. You might think that is all very tame now, but at that time, it was like going on stage on the moon.

JK: I saw that tour, and I had never seen anything like it in my life. I was about 15, and I remember thinking, *Wow!*

SH: Weren't we crazy to take all this other stuff? When I met Julian Bream through the great John Williams, he came up to me and said, "Are you the guitarist with three trucks?" That was a phenomenal question because he couldn't understand how a guitarist could have three trucks worth of equipment. Obviously I was in Yes, and there was a keyboard player and there was a bass player, etc. and he couldn't comprehend how we could have three trucks. But of course, the PA was in one, the backline was in the other, and the production was in the third. Of course, this was nothing compared to ELP. And take Pink Floyd going out with eighty trucks! So we were small fry, really.

In a way, sadly, Yes have always been the underdogs, you know? This has made us fight long and hard and come back many, many times. You might not think that is fair. Critically we are not really underdogs, even though we have been slagged off and been called rock dinosaurs and that kind of thing, which I took in my stride although Rick Wakeman didn't. It didn't matter what people said; we are who we are. We have always been a working band, rarely do people retire from Yes because we have always been just below the big or biggest picture, so there might still be things we will do that will elevate us to the higher ambition. We are ambitious, and we have never reached the top point of our ambition.

JK: I said to Tony Kaye once that being in Yes is a bit like being in part of the secret service – no-one is allowed to leave! If you do, it kind of comes and follows you around.

SH: Yes. Everyone has a reference that they were in Yes once, or they are currently in Yes, or they are no longer in Yes, or ex-Yes.

JK: *Close To The Edge* was the final one with Bill Bruford. I have spoken to him about this, and he said that at the time, he felt that he was never going to be able to top what he had done playing on that album. For him, that was the top album that he could ever play on with Yes and felt that it was time for him to go. Were you surprised when Bill decided to leave?

SH: Well, I was horrified, and shocked, and devastated, more than I could believe. Strangely enough, drummers have always had an essential role in groups I have played in. The first drummer I ever played with was called Johnny Melton in Syndicats, and we spoke last year sometime. We hadn't stayed in touch for about 40 years, and we got back in touch through the internet. I remember looking on stage with the Syndicats and looking at him. I didn't use to look at the audience, but the drummer, because the physical actions he did produced the sound I needed to be hooked into. When I first went down to Barnes to play with Yes on the audition day, if you can call it that, I walked in, we started playing, and I looked at Bill. I couldn't take my eyes off him. I thought it was amazing, astounding drumming, and of course, I wanted to play in this band. Even if I didn't like anyone else in the group, I still wanted to play with Yes. (*Laughs*) As it happened, I loved all of the players and the people. It was a total hit with me.

Apparently, it was Bill who said to them cautiously afterwards that this Steve Howe was a bit of a hippie! But I think prog only happened because of psychedelia. You see, it enabled them to do whatever the hell they liked. That was my meal ticket. That was what I wanted from music forevermore after that. Before that, I had been in a pop band and an R&B band, a blues band.

I had done those things, and suddenly, I was in a band where I could invent. I could help to invent what this band was like. I could actually get my ideas into it! I could use my guitar, I could overdub – I was a fantasiser, and so was everybody else. When we got into the studio, it was really a question of: "Which idea are we going to follow now?" When we talked about "And You and I," remarkable things happened on there.

In Europe, they released the wrong version. Did you ever hear about this? On the album called *The Ultimate Yes*, which they had rush-released to meet with our tour in Europe, they mistakenly put the wrong "And You and I" on it. This indicates not only how stupid labels can be, but also, they couldn't find tapes, some of which they got from me eventually for *In A Word: Yes*. In the rush to release the album, they used the wrong tape. We had another ending on it where we went "amen" for a very long time, and that is what is available! In the studio, we had been working on the song. We did not like the ending. We didn't like "amen," as we thought it was a bit corny, even though the "ah" bit did last an awfully long time. So, we went back in and recut the endings. This shows we weren't done until the fat lady had sung, you know. It had to go on until we felt we couldn't improve it any more. "And You And I" is a spectacularly recorded piece, and it still sounds good. In the 70s, I was listening to the American group The Byrds, thinking, *God, it's ten years old, and it sounds that good!* And now when I hear that album, it was the same with that record. I still think it sounds that good. The Byrds still sound great of course, "Eight Miles High" for instance; any of their songs are spectacular.

So I am very proud that *The Yes Album* was hiatus really because *Topographic Oceans* wasn't made under those circumstances. It would take a while to discuss that album, but it was a bit more difficult. And of course, Eddie did that album as well. But up to then, Eddie's creativity was great, and Eddie and I would go, "Well we like this here, how are we going to do that? Well, we could put it on that machine and then tie it back and slide this in…" So we started trying things round on the songs and arrange it and fix them in a way. We were techno minded. I didn't just get it from Eddie; I had worked with Joe Meek and other producers and found production really interesting.

When I first got home with *The Yes Album* and put it on a mono record player, which was all I had at the time. When we finished that, I thought to myself, *What the hell have we made here? What does this sound like?* It was all so new that even I did not realise what the total effect of us playing like that, with that kind of sound and that kind of production, was actually going to sound like. Only when I got home, I realised. I thought it was incredibly quirky, *The Yes Album*. It was like, "What kind of band is this? Who do they think they are?" I can hear all those things going through my mind, "Why is it like that? Do we really sound like that?" But of course, it was enjoyed in America, Europe, and England, so much that it won its own credibility.

JK: There are so many legendary stories about the track "Close To The Edge." It was done a piece at a time, and I think all the work that went into it paid off because not only the track, but the album is one of those great headphones albums, where you hear new stuff all the time on the headphones.

SH: Absolutely. There are places where the live show has never been the same. When you get to near the end of the song, and we return to the final "Close to the edge..." there is no guitar playing there. I don't know what happened. I didn't like the original there, and I never replaced it. It did get hard to work on a piece that was twenty minutes long. A lot of it was played live, and the great thing about it is the beginning is all live work; it is added to with a guitar harmony or a guitar octave here and there. Then Rick added the keyboards, which were really complicated, and nice movements all implied by the bass, guitar, and drums. It was all live, and the stuff was quite tightly arranged. But it was still free, as well. I remember Jon and I talking about the beginning, and he suggested that just for a change, it should start with improvisation. We just looked at each other and said, "Wow, that is adventurous." So that is why it comes out of nowhere, and we were just going nuts. I love everything about the *Close To The Edge* album. I love the shape; I love the feel of it.

JK: It is hard to do something and not repeat yourself, though? You just don't want to repeat yourself, do you?

SH: It wouldn't be good enough to repeat ourselves. It would have to start with the writing and arranging. Before you get to the record, you have to already know an awful lot about it. You can do that in Pro Tools – build pictures, positions, placements, and lengths. But the way we did it was very much piecemeal, and there had to be a song written somewhere.

JK: How did you feel when you first had to go out and perform this live? I believe that you launched *Close To The Edge* at a concert at Chrystal Palace. Again, not only are you playing a really long and involved piece of music, but you have also got a new drummer!

SH: I know, I did brush over too quickly on that subject before. You asked me how I felt, and yes, I was devastated that Bill wanted to go because I loved him so much. I wanted him to stay. But then I got very shirty with Bill and said to him that if he wanted to go, he ought to go now and not do another tour. That is the worst thing I ever said to Bill. Now, we are still friends; it did not spoil our friendship. But at the time, I felt that if he was not committed to the group, he should not do any more but just move on. Everybody else picked up on the sentiment, only apparently because that is what happened. He didn't go on the tour even though he offered to do the tour, and I regret that so much. I don't think I have ever confessed this so openly before. Although I have told that story before, I have never added to it that it would have been great for him to go on the tour, because I wouldn't want it to reflect badly on Alan.

JK: Bill told me that the first time he played *Close To The Edge* was when Anderson, Bruford, Wakeman Howe went out. He said that he had fun learning it. He had to listen to it and then thought, *Ah yes, I remember this now!* But he did have fun learning it for that tour because he had never played it before.

SH: Yeah, that's astounding, isn't it? I have to say that when ABWH played anything from *Close To The Edge*, it was phenomenal because Tony Levin played it just like the record. Over the years, Chris has liked to stretch things and change them, and all that was gone. We were playing *Close To The Edge* more like the original *Close To The Edge* than ever before. There were no changes; Tony had really learned it like the record.

JK: On the live version of the record, Jeff Berlin came in, and Bill said he was very impressed. He said that he was so impressed that he loved telling people how impressed he was that Jeff came in and literally learned the entire set in just a couple of days.

SH: That's right! He did a beautiful, beautiful job. But he didn't do two things: he didn't replace Chris Squire, and he didn't replace Tony Levin. He kind of found himself a new way of doing it that was very individual but didn't have some of the elements we were used to with Tony because he was fantastic on stage and very kind of spooky to watch. Jeff is very much a top-flight musician – very much.

JK: You were in the band until 1980, and then you left when the band kind of fell apart. But really, if you think about it, when the band reconstituted, you and Geoff were in Asia. It wasn't really that much later. Did you miss being in Yes, or were you too focussed on Asia?

SH: Well, the way that the band fell apart needs a simple bit of clarity. There was no reason to break up at that point, but there was a disharmony where

Chris and Alan wanted to experiment with some other music, and Trevor had the commitment to do the second Buggles album, although that also applied to Geoff too. Then it turned out that Geoff and I were left sitting in a room saying, "Do you want to carry on with Yes?" In a way, the other three couldn't foresee it. Trevor's feeling was that if we weren't going to support him as a vocalist, then he wasn't going to stay. So, we did have a difficult but interesting thing to do. I told Geoff that I had just spent ten years chopping and changing with all these people, and I couldn't do it anymore. But within two months, I had met John Wetton and started the first waves of Asia, if you like. Yes started being called Cinema with Chris and Trevor Rabin, and it was only in the last minute before they released it that they got Jon back to sing on it, and they called it Yes. I was really chuffed that Asia had got off the ground so well. I didn't know that it was going to fall apart only a year or so later. But I was so chuffed that it was doing well that it boosted my confidence completely. I thought, *Well, I had a hit with Yes and I had a hit with Asia*, and this was going kind of well. I was looking down my nose a bit and listening to a little bit of what Yes were doing, and then they were vastly successful, so I had to be much more considerate in my views on them. Of course, there were a lot of trademarks still going on in the sound with Chris and Jon, of course, and that was still evident. But then they took forever to do *Big Generator*. When they did that, I started to think, *Well however much I am switching groups…* and I have got GTR now. By the time they brought out *Big Generator*, I was in GTR with Steve Hackett, once again, not knowing that it was going to be another short experience.

So, lo and behold, we had ABWH, which brought us around full circle back with Tony Levin because that again only lasted one album. We started the second album, and that became *Union*. The 80s were a mixed-up jingle jangle of a career for me, but many of them were very powerful, as Asia was and still is a contender since we came back in 2006. It's been a contender with me all the time, and now Geoff has come back into Yes, so we are in an unusual weird crossover stage between Yes and Asia, but they are very distinct. There is never any chance that Yes will sound like Asia and Asia will sound like Yes because Geoff and I play differently in each group. And that is its strength; it has a different calling.

JK: There was a massive amount of success for Yes in the 80s, although I think without *Drama*, I don't think there would have been as much success in the 80s. For me personally, I wasn't such a big fan of *Tormato*, but when I heard *Drama*, I thought it was much more like Yes.

SH: That's right, and I was exactly the same way with *Tormato*. I have criticised the album a lot; not the individuals, but the sound and the texture of the playing. It wasn't really working very well. I remember Ahmet coming in when we were playing "Release Release," and him saying, "Is the rest of the album that good?" And I said, "Yes!" I think that was an outstanding track. But *Tormato* was really a torment, not only with the sleeve design. Like *Going For The One*, it was, "Why are we doing this? Why don't we have Roger?" But Roger was not popular with a certain member of the band, and therefore we lost Roger for a while. He came back with *Drama*, but as you say, without *Drama*, the end of the 70s would have been quite a let-down, because *Tormato* wasn't cohesive. It was interesting and very complicated...probably too complicated. We've never played the opening pieces since then, and I don't particularly want to. They're quite nice, but I don't know what they are. As you say with *Drama*, we have been recently playing "Machine Messiah" and "Tempus Fugit." They are great pieces, and it is an astounding album! It did make me feel they changed the guitar sound, and that was a respectable thing to do; they camped it up a bit.

I do laugh when I see the "Owner Of A Lonely Heart" video immensely. There are all sorts of people that drop in and out of that, that aren't really a part of it. They did take a long time to do two albums, although admittedly, they did do *Talk* after *Union*, and they decided to break up the *Union* line-up. It wasn't anything to do with Rick, Bill, or me, but we put up with it and realised that we had lost ABWH, which to us at that time was a feasibly reasonable group. We could have had many songs from *Union* on our second album, which was *ABWH II*, and it would have been partly what *Union* had to offer.

JK: Bill seems to think it was the record company that killed off ABWH. Is that what you think?

SH: Well, there was some deal at the time, which we didn't know about, whereby if ABWH could become Yes, then there would be some sort of deal on the table. What it meant, of course, was that Atlantic had to sell the rights to Yes over to Arista. So, it was a preposterous, stupid, unnecessary idea, particularly because although Arista was prepared to have a second album from Yes after *Union*, the guys wouldn't listen to advice, which was quite simply: don't do this altogether in one room. Let's have different line-ups working together, like Jon and me; but that all went wrong. So, when I look at that period of time, as good as they were, they didn't produce that much music and didn't come up with an album every year or so, which would have put them on the map.

JK: Do you think it was a lost opportunity with ABWH, then? Bill had said that when you were down in the South of France with Bill, preparing to work on the second ABWH album before the *Union* project, you, Bill, and Tony Levin were jamming on some material. And he thought it sounded incredible, and then the management came and pulled the rug from underneath you and told you that you would be doing the *Union* project. Bill seemed a bit disappointed. How did you feel?

SH: Yeah, I agree completely with what Bill said, and Rick was on the same page as us. This was a disaster because of this *Union* idea. But we thought we were going to carry on with ABWH after *Union*, but they had a different idea. But the bit you are talking about from ABWH through to *Union* by Yes…that was a difficult time. But things had got a little difficult in the writing process too because Rick and Bill don't write Yes music as much as Jon and Chris and I have done over the years, even though they are both capable of writing for Yes, and have done so over the years. But no matter how difficult it was during all this, it was even difficult to get Jon and me together too. Jonathan Elias was a mixed blessing too. It is alright having enthusiasm, but it needs methods of work and methods that work well, and there was a lot of over-recording. Stuff happened on that album, and I know Rick has been scathing about the album, so some things are better left forgotten. But I am hoping one day that Arista will say, "Why don't you remix that album and make it the way it should have been?" (*Laughs*) But who knows.

JK: The thing about Yes, and forgive me for saying this, but I feel I can as a fan of long-standing: there has never been an easy way for Yes. Or at least that's how it seems as someone outside looking in. However, I do have access to privileged information, as to the running of Yes, as I have known all you guys a long time. So as a musician, does that frustrate you sometimes?

SH: Yes it does, of course. The thing is, even now if you look at it, we still have a lot of baggage that goes back. So as much as we want to be a new group – and we have Jon Davison singing, and he is fantastic, and we are really happy and can move forward now – we have this 45-year trail behind us, and it is almost the breakdown of business understanding. If you could imagine that musicians are completely innocent, with regards to business and money, then you would be silly, but we see a lot of other people between us that has made a lot of mess, and that does slow us down. So we have to be more conscious of expenditure and be not quite as extravagant, which is what we have been blamed for. We get told, "It's your own fault and your own doing," but there were degrees of extravagance. No one could ever call Bill extravagant. He may have been tarnished with the same brush, but he definitely wasn't extravagant. So, these are some of the problems caused, and some of them are still with us, of course, but that is as much as I can say, really.

JK: There was a big controversy when Jon left in 1979, and then Trevor Horn and Geoff Downes came in. You kind of rode that out as a band but did eventually end up splitting. But again, for me personally, I think all the criticism was unjustified. The album had a Roger Dean sleeve, Eddie Offord was involved, albeit briefly, and the vocals did sound like "Yes" vocals, so it did sound like a Yes album.

SH: Precisely.

JK: Presumably the way is forward now, (and bear in mind, I have only seen Jon Davison with the band on YouTube), but I prefer to see the bigger picture and see Yes as a band, rather than a group of individuals. And I think the people that get into the thing of who is in the band or isn't in the band are missing out on a lot.

SH: Well, there is a tendency to do that. And sometimes even past members voice their opinions and say, "You should do it this way," or, "You shouldn't do it that way." But a lot of people need reminding that there is only one way you can have this: and that is the way that Chris, Alan, and I have pushed it on since 2008. It is indicative of what we did with Jon from 1996 to 2004, and that was to actually elevate Yes by doing great shows. It is the only thing we can do, and the only way we can better ourselves is by being better. So if you take that view, I think what Yes is doing now is quite astounding, and I can step outside of Yes for a moment and think, *Yeah, this is the 45th year next year.* I like playing any of the material, say from *Time And A Word* to *Keys To Ascension*, and even *90125*. I don't mind what we do, because I am constantly thinking about that bigger picture.

I have my personal take on it and how Yes is helping my career generally when I go to Asia or play with my trio. At one time, I was doing lots of solo shows, and I want to do that again, but it all helps me. Then again, I help Yes. I am happy to make music with Yes and music without Yes. So, I am more versatile, but I do appreciate the importance of Yes. But the fans seeing it in different ways will happen, and there will be people who will voice their opinions, usually when they have seen us recently with Jon Davison. I sat next to Jon every night on the meet and greets, and most people were saying things like, "It was incredible," and some even said, "I wasn't even thinking of Jon or Benoit." So, if we can bring about things like that, then I think there is an incredible future still.

JK: There is a lot of talk about a new album, so you must be pleased that there has been a positive response to the band talking about a new album.

SH: Well, *Fly From Here* was our new album, and that was talked about before we did it, so I don't want to talk too much about a new album just yet. I don't feel the need to be rushed about this, although I know Frontiers are keen for another album. But we need to get the game up, and Trevor helped us a lot with the last one. We don't know where we are going with the next one yet. We don't know what kind of record it will be.

JK: How do you see Yes going forward then? Seeing as next year is the band's 45th Anniversary, it must be exciting for you.

SH: I think it is fantastic, and I hope we can do something fantastic. I think we have shown recently by bringing in "America" and "Awaken" that we can bring back material that really pleases our fans. We closed most nights with "Awaken," and people were coming up saying "That *IS* my favourite Yes song!" And while a lot of people like "Close To The Edge," "Awaken" is a standout song. So, if we keep doing that, I know we have creative ideas for the kind of show we want to do. And that isn't about having production and scenery; it's about what we play. (*Laughs*) Although, I think we're expected to have something going on, and we do because we have projections and stuff going on. We have an adequate production going on, I think, because I am interested as a musician that stands there and plays, and that is more where I come from. I like a bit of rock n rolling occasionally and have a bit of fun, but I prefer Yes to be a little more serious. So I lean a little bit on the studious and serious side, so that is where the music is indicative of my view.

JK: Well in closing, whenever I hear "And You And I," I am always transported back to a time when I was 14 years old and first got into Yes. So the question is, do you have any moments as a musician with the band, when you are playing some of the songs, and they take you back to the time and what you were doing when you first came up with the song or first played it?

SH: Well, when you are doing it, you can't think about what you're thinking about. Thoughts kind of wander through your mind, but you aren't really in that domain much because your mind, while you are on stage, is in a semi kind of blank stage, and you are very much hooked into the music. But when I hear the music or when I am practising it at home, then that's when it happens, although those memories are always with me. It's like when I spoke about *The Yes Album* – that area of Devon became entrenched within my personality because of the two months I spent there writing and playing the music. I believe there is a lot of crossing over in these emotions all the time.

My wife Jan and I have been together over 40 years, so we have known this music also, so my wife is a big part of it, and my four kids are a big part of it. It is all part of the same thing; it's not easy to separate it. Sometimes just before I go on stage, I think I'm a guitarist, and I'm going to go onstage. Now I actually get to do what it is I do. And the other thing is, say at the beginning of a song like "And You And I," it only takes a few seconds, but I compose myself and then think, *Okay*, and then I start playing it. And quite often we get a reaction, which is great, and dealing with that is emotional; the memories it has for them and for me. It is a great memory field mixed in with the practical and sonic considerations.

Steve Howe celebrated his 42nd Anniversary with Yes in the summer of 2012. There was a period in the 80s when he was not a member of Yes, but a member of Asia – the band that grew out of the then-split Yes in late 1980. Steve was also involved in a group project with former Genesis guitarist Steve Hackett called GTR in 1985. In early 2013, Steve Howe announced his departure from Asia in order to concentrate on his solo projects and Yes. Steve and Geoff Downes are now both current members of Yes, and are embarking on Yes' 45th Anniversary tour in March 2013. They are set to perform *The Yes Album*, *Close To The Edge*, and *Going For the One* in their entireties.

Update 2019

Steve Howe is still very much part of Yes and continues to lead the band musically, as he has for all his time in the band. Never content to rest on the collective laurels the band has earned, Steve pushes the band on to even greater musical heights. In 2017, Steve was inducted into the Rock n Roll Hall of Fame as part of Yes.

∼

Jon Davison: The New Singer In Yes
October 2012

In late 2011, Yes were on the European leg of their world tour to promote the band's most recent album, *Fly From Here*. The band had enjoyed an upswing in fortunes with the release of the album, which had garnered good reviews. The subsequent live dates, which had, at this point, covered America and the UK, had also received very good positive reviews. Shortly after the Manchester date in late November, Benoit David started to experience problems with his breathing, making singing difficult. The situation persisted until the dates in Russia, where Benoit was unable to continue with the tour, resulting in the last two dates being cancelled.

The initial idea was for Benoit to take time off and recover, but when it became apparent that Benoit would not be fit enough for the dates in New Zealand, Australia, and Japan in April 2013, the band (with the agreement of Benoit), opted to find a replacement. Initially it was to cover the dates in the Far East, but subsequently, Jon Davison (who had been recommended to Chris Squire by the Foo Fighters' Taylor Hawkins), became a permanent member. Jon had previously sung with the Yes tribute band Roundabout, and also had a background of fronting his own band, Sky Cries Mary. Since 2009, Jon has also been the vocalist for Glass Hammer, and has recorded three albums with them: *If*, *Cor Cordium*, and *Perilous*. Here is how Jon Davison describes his first six months in Yes.

Jon Kirkman (JK): You have been in Yes just over six months now. How does it feel fronting one of the great rock bands of the last 45 years?

Jon Davison (JD): Seeing as Yes has always been one of my favourite bands, you can imagine the high I feel performing side by side with them on stage. It's truly a surreal experience!

JK: Let's go back a little while before you joined Yes. We know you are a member of Glass Hammer, and the band are about to release their latest album, which is your third album with the band. How did you come to join Glass Hammer, who also have a strong fan-base like Yes?

JD: Fred and Steve found me online singing live with the Yes tribute act

Roundabout in a YouTube video. I was initially invited to sing lead on only one song – a remake of "Long And Long Ago" (The Inconsolable Secret). Then they asked if I would track vocals on a couple more tunes from the same project. After working together for a few months and mutually enjoying the productive and creative chemistry, the guys invited me to join as lead vocalist, and help collaborate on material for what was to become the next album, which eventually became *If*.

JK: When did you start out in music, so to speak? What are the other main bands you have been in, and what style of music did they play?

JD: My first professional gig was on bass guitar with Sky Cries Mary, followed by performing as lead vocalist in Roundabout. The first instrument I picked up at age 14 was the electric guitar. My best friend who lived up the road was a drummer, and we enthusiastically formed our first band in the fifth or sixth grade. His name is Taylor Hawkins, who, as we all know, has made quite a name for himself.

JK: Obviously, being a member of two groups requires great coordination with schedules and calendars. Are you finding that an easy thing to accommodate?

JD: So far so good, as I knock on wood!

JK: It is no secret that you were the singer with a Yes tribute band, Roundabout. Do you occasionally have a look around on stage and see the other guys from Yes and think, *Wow! How did I get here?* I think many people could understand if you did.

JD: Yeah, that has happened on numerous occasions. Sharing the stage night after night with some of my greatest heroes, and having the privilege of getting to know them as the good souls they are, has all been so amazing!

JK: Let's look at the current situation. First of all, who made the first approach, and how was that approach made? Were you aware that Benoit had been ill and couldn't make the tour?

JD: I was first contacted by their manager Paul Silveira, who was already aware of my singing with Glass Hammer. My wife Maewe and I had also met Paul a few years before at a Syn show. Up until the time of his call, I was unaware that Benoit was struggling.

JK: Was the original offer made to cover just the upcoming dates at the time in New Zealand, Australia and Japan? Or was there a firm offer straight away?

JD: Yes, the initial agreement was that I would only help them through the upcoming dates.

JK: When was the offer made to become a full member of Yes? Was it just after the tour? What was your reaction to that? How does it feel being an "Official" member of Yes? Do you have any say in setlists, etc.?

JD: It was never formally said, just understood. Yes, I'm able to give input for the setlists.

JK: How much rehearsal did you undertake for the tour?

JD: Aside from personal preparation, I had about five rehearsals with the band.

JK: In terms of the rehearsals, can you remember the set that was suggested by the band that you had to learn? Were there any songs that you were worried about? What was the first song you sang with the band?

JD: The first song we rehearsed was "I've Seen All Good People." I was already familiar with most of the material at the time the set was proposed. I knew that as long as I was diligent in doing my homework, there wouldn't be anything to worry about. Let that be a lesson to the kids out there – DO YOUR HOMEWORK!

JK: Having accepted the role to sing with Yes, you must have been aware that there was going to be a lot of attention on you as the latest frontman for the band. Did that add to the pressure, or where you okay with that? How has that worked out between you and the fans?

JD: As long as I'm delivering musically, I can relax and trust that for the most part, the rest will take care of itself. I really enjoy meeting and connecting with friends and fans of the band. We share a common affection for the music. I feel that I'm up there on stage for all of us.

JK: The reviews overall have been incredibly positive, and many reviewers have singled you out for praise, including many from the Yes fan base. That must be confirmation for you, and also nice to know that you are doing a good job.

JD: Absolutely.

JK: How quickly did the set come together for the tour? Were there any major differences between singing for a tribute band and singing for the real thing? The reason I ask is because some tribute bands are more exacting in their tribute to the band. So was it as you expected it to be?

JD: I remember the set coming together swiftly. They were appreciative of the fact that I was so prepared. Performing the music with the musicians that actually created it is a singular experience above singing in a band that can only pay tribute. There's an intuitive connection between a musician and the music that has originated through them.

JK: Benoit said there were obvious favourites he enjoyed singing with the band; his personal favourite being "Onward." But there were also a couple of songs he had difficulty with, "Parallels" and "Going For The One". Are there any songs in the set that you would be wary of tackling, or are you fine with anything the band has come up with so far? Your voice suggests that the majority of the Yes catalogue would be well within your range.

JD: So far, there hasn't been a song to come up that I'm wary of.

JK: Can you remember how it felt waiting to go on stage at the first date in Auckland? How did you think the gig went at the time?

JD: Rehearsals had gone very well, and as a result, I had already gained the confidence of the band. This gave me all the assurance I needed to confidently go out onstage. I thought the show was a real success.

JK: Yes have never played New Zealand before, so was there any more pressure in addition to being the first gig with the band?

JD: No. In fact, it relaxed me a bit, knowing that my first gig with the band was, in a way, also a first for them.

JK: Do you have any overriding memories from the tour of New Zealand, Australia, and Japan?

JD: I had been to Tokyo once before in the 90s while touring with Sky Cries Mary. I have always found the people of Japan to be so kind and respectful, and the same qualities were expressed again during this last tour with Yes. I remember how my wife Maewe and I were both lovingly welcomed by Yes fans in New Zealand and Australia. In fact, everywhere we've toured: Indonesia, Canada, Mexico, and throughout the United States, including Hawaii. Fans everywhere are remembered for their many acts of kindness expressed toward us.

JK: When was it made official that you were going to be the new full-time vocalist for the band?

JD: Yes never used the term "official," but I'm definitely the new singer.

JK: Having toured with the band in New Zealand, Australia, and Japan, how did you approach the American tour this summer?

JD: I approached it much the same way, but with a greater sense of confidence.

JK: With the band wanting to promote the *Fly From Here* album and songs from the album in the set, was it any easier than it was singing some of the classics like "Heart Of The Sunrise," or "And You And I?" I realise that either way, you are singing songs that someone else has sung, but the classics have been established for over 40 years, in some cases, whereas *Fly From Here* is still establishing itself.

JD: The *Fly From Here* material ended up being equally as challenging but in a different kind of way. A lot of the vocal parts are in a lower register than what I was accustomed to at the time. I now feel at home with those parts, and really enjoy performing the material. As you said, the songs from *Fly From Here* are still being established within the live context, and therefore I'm able to put a bit more of my own interpretive spin on them. I've had a lot of fun throughout the process.

JK: Has the set changed significantly over the last six months?

JD: I'd say the bulk of the set has remained the same. But some selections were dropped so that we could bring in fresh material, most of which had not been performed by the band for quite some time.

JK: Can you give me some examples of what has been dropped and what has been added? Also, how would you feel tackling material from, say, *Topographic Oceans* or *Relayer*? Is there anything, in particular, you would like to see Yes perform?

JD: I would love to bring to the stage selections from either *Topographic Oceans* or *Relayer*. In fact, during this last tour, Steve and I had already touched on this by adding "Leaves Of Green" as a duet to his acoustic section.

JK: After the summer tour of America, your thoughts now must be looking forward to the next album, which Chris Squire has said the band are keen to record next year with you as a full member of the band. Have you had any ideas for songs yet, or perhaps lyrics?

JD: Yes, I have offered both music and lyrics. Some collaboration has occurred as well.

JK: Next year is the band's 45th Anniversary, so any album the band releases will be an important one. We are back to talking pressure again, really. How do you feel approaching the recording of the next album?

JD: Each album is the one and only important album at the particular time of its conception. At this stage, the significant thing for me is that my ideas have been received graciously and with enthusiasm. I'm now looking forward to the next step of further collaboration between members. I won't allow my creative process to be about pressure, which is stifling. It is and will continue to be about inspiration.

JK: Looking back on the last year, what are your feelings about the turn of events that has brought you to fronting one of the world's biggest rock bands?

JD: I'm grateful for the opportunity to front one of my most beloved bands. It's an honour to be instrumental in helping them to carry on.

JK: What are you looking forward to in the next 12 months with Yes?

JD: More adventures on the road, spending time together as friends, and feeling the music between us and the audiences. I look forward to collaborative efforts and sharing the musical journey of discovery for the new album.

JK: You are about to start promotion on the new Glass Hammer album *Perilous*, and then after Christmas, you're back with Yes in the early part of the year celebrating the band's 45th Anniversary. This will include the Cruise To The Edge event with both Glass Hammer and Yes headlining. Would it be fair to say that things for you now, personally, are pretty good?

JD: YES! (Pun intended!)

Moving into 2013, Jon Davison fronts Yes and takes the band into their 45th year, which is bound to be a busy year; both in a celebratory way, and hopefully a creative way with more live shows. Plus, there's the potential of a new album, which would be the band's 21st studio album, and Jon Davison's first with the band. In addition to that, there is also Jon's work with Glass Hammer, who released their latest album *Perilous*, which was their third album with Jon, in late 2012.

∾

Oliver Wakeman: A Family Thing
August 2012

When Yes announced in 2008 that the band would be celebrating their 40th Anniversary after a four-year hiatus, the Yes fan base was incredibly happy. There would be a tour, and possibly an album ahead of the tour. The line-up would be Anderson, Squire, Howe, White, and Wakeman, although the Wakeman in question was to be Oliver Wakeman, rather than Rick Wakeman, who decided not to tour with the band. Oliver was officially announced as the latest member of Yes in early 2008, and all was going well. The tour was announced, and everything was being prepared until on the 13th of May. Jon Anderson suffered a severe asthma attack, and at one point, his life was even in danger. Happily, Jon Anderson recovered, although he would not immediately be able to fulfil his professional responsibilities to Yes.

The tour was cancelled, and everyone thought that would be the end of the tour until Jon Anderson recovered. The band, however, decided not to wait for Anderson to recover and engaged Benoit David to fill the vocalist slot with Oliver Wakeman still on-board. Over the next three years, Oliver played 150 concerts with the band, recorded a live album and DVD, which was released in late 2010, and contributed to the preparation and early days of the studio album that would eventually be released as *Fly From Here*. In early 2011, however, Oliver was out of Yes and off the album, not without some drama...no pun intended.

Jon Kirkman (JK): Oliver, as many people know, you were a member of Yes between 2008 and 2010, but let me take you back a fair way before that. How old were you when you discovered that your father didn't have a normal nine to five job, and he was a musician with Yes?

Oliver Wakeman (OW): Well, if I go right back to the age of about five, my Mum and Dad divorced, so he wasn't about much, really, until I was about twelve because he was touring heavily. I was born in 1972, so around the time of *Fragile*. In fact, it was just after *Fragile* because in the books I was mentioned as the one future offspring in the booklet with the album. So, when *Fragile* took off, Dad was touring all the time. When I got to the age of about five, which is the age where you become aware of what is going on around your family, my Mum and Dad had divorced. He went to live in Switzerland, so I didn't get to see him for a long time. So, by the time I was getting older, instead of it being something quite special – it was the 80s, remember – bands like Yes were not really in vogue at all; I used to get teased about it a bit. So, it was only in my late teens when my friends were discovering bands like Yes that suddenly it became very cool.

JK: Was it a given that you would become a musician, or did you have ambitions elsewhere?

OW: Not really. It was never encouraged, let's put it that way. It was just something I enjoyed doing, and my brother also enjoyed playing as well, so I think it was just a natural progression. I think you have a genetic ability or understanding of how to play the piano, and by hard work and practice and learning how to do it, you become good at it. Then you suddenly realise that it makes it more appealing as a career.

JK: I first became aware of you as an artist through the two albums you recorded with Clive Nolan, who of course, is the keyboard player with Arena and Pendragon. You played a big part in both *Jabberwocky* and *Hound Of The Baskervilles*.

OW: Well, I tried to pull those albums into a different kind of direction. I think Clive wrote some of his best material on those two albums.

JK: I was also aware of the album you made with Steve Howe, *The Three Ages Of Magick*. How did that collaboration come about?

OW: Well, that was an album that basically I wrote, and the way it came about was quite by chance. My Mum lives in Devon, and as you may know, Steve has a house in North Devon, and I was hitchhiking. A friend of mine had given me a ticket that got me part of the way down there, and I had to hitchhike the rest of the way. So I got off the train at Tiverton and Steve was standing on the platform. I went over to him and said, "Hello, Steve!" and he looked at me like, *Who Are You?* and I said, "I'm Oliver, Rick's son." Since I had hung out on the ABWH tour, he recognised me and offered me a lift part of the way down to my Mum's.

We bumped into each other again sometime later, just after I had released my first album, and I was stood outside a record shop. He asked me what I was doing, and I was actually stood next to a poster for the album. So I said, "Well, I'm doing this now." He asked me to send him a copy, and he rang me up after he had heard it. He said he liked it and started to invite me over to his house where we would talk about music and play stuff together. With some of the stuff I played, he asked me what I was going to do with it, and I said I was going to be making another album. It was at that point that Steve suggested that he would like to be an executive producer and play on it and produce it. So, I was happy for him to do that. I wrote some music, and then he would send some parts to it. We would discuss tracks, and really that was how it got done. We had some fun making the album.

JK: It got some very good reviews, as I recall.

OW: Yeah. In fact, every review I read of the album was positive, except for this one review from the local newspaper in Devon that hated it! (*Laughs*) It went something like, "Technically great, and you can't fault the music, but I don't want to sit at the Druid's table that often."

JK: I take it you no longer buy that paper anymore.

OW: (*Laughs*) No, not at all. I think I kept the review, though.

JK: Well, when you joined Yes, I remember thinking that was a very obvious move, but then, on the other hand, it must have been a little strange for you. Was that the case?

OW: It was terrifying, actually. I joined at the same time as Benoit. I remember turning up at the very first rehearsal, which was in Hamilton, Ontario, Canada. Bear in mind, I had never played with Yes before, and contrary to popular belief, I had never sat down and worked out any Yes music before. Everybody imagined my Dad had sat me down and taught me to play all these songs, which of course he hadn't. So I had to listen to all the records, work out all the parts, and then turn up in Canada with a brand new keyboard rig and new keyboard technician, and just have ten days to rehearse a three and a half-hour set before the first show.

JK: Surely, that is a good thing though, as you don't have too much time to dwell on things. As I recall, that was the way your Dad had to learn the set when he replaced Tony Kaye.

OW: That's more than likely, but I just remembered thinking it was such a big job to take on. You must remember, when my Dad joined, he was just learning the music from three albums. I was having to learn a great deal more and also learning music that my Dad had written. You look at the setlist, and when you see the setlist and think that "Heart Of The Sunrise" is one of the easier tracks to learn, you know you are in trouble! (*Laughs*) It was a bit pressured. I knew that the minute I walked out on stage because I was replacing my Dad, I would be under even more scrutiny. Since Benoit had been in a Yes tribute band prior, he knew three-quarters of the set off the top of his head, so he had a bit of a lead on me.

JK: I suppose as well, due to the circumstances, there will always be an element of the audience that will think, *Impress me.*

OW: Oh, yeah. I had two views when I started. The first was that I wrote to my Dad and said, "Look, I'm doing this, and I don't know how much you had to do with this, but I don't want it to become an issue but do I have your blessing to do this?" And he wrote back and said, "Of course you do." So, that was one thing. The second was, I couldn't get up on stage and do what he did, in that he amends things and changes things as he plays them. But I thought, *I haven't earned the right to do that,* so I went back to the way that the songs sounded on the albums. I played them exactly like they had been played on the record, which Dad never did live. For instance, the solo on "And You And I" had not been played as it was on the record since the album had been recorded. So, little things like that were the things that I thought I could bring to the band. That and also a little authenticity; make the keyboards sound like they did on the albums, and stuff like that. I think that it was only when the live album came out that I am on that people could see how hard I had worked at trying to bring that authenticity to the band. And when they did realise that it was quite nice.

JK: Who was it that made the initial approach for you to be in the band? Was it the management, or one of the guys in the band?

OW: It was actually Steve Howe that rang me. He actually rang me up ten months before I joined the band because of course, I was meant to join the band and tour when Jon Anderson was still in the band before he was taken ill. So when he rang me and asked me if I wanted to join, I just spoke to my wife briefly and said, "Yes!" But then Jon became ill, and I didn't really know what was going to happen.

JK: Did you ever rehearse with Jon, or did his illness happen before rehearsals could start? What was the situation?

OW: Well, it was strange because I actually had a job, which I did between projects in music. I quit my job because the tour was starting in the June or whatever, and I was working my notice. I had I think about two or three days left before I left to head off for the pre-tour rehearsals. And then I got this email from Jon saying, "I'm sick, it's not going to happen." So I thought, *Okay, what am I going to do now?* My whole life had been turned around because I was going to join Yes. My house was on the market and my wife, and I had a young son, and she wanted to be close to her parents if I was off travelling around the world. As you can imagine, this email comes out of the blue, and I had to stop and think, *Well, what do I do now?* (*Laughs*)

Well, I had to take the house off the market and not leave the job, but then about three months after that, I got another phone call from Steve, and he basically said, "It's not announced yet, but we've got somebody else we're going to use instead of Jon. Do you still want to join the band?" So, having gone through all the sacrifices and still thinking that it would be a great opportunity, I just switched everything back on again. If I am totally honest, I was very glad to get to that first rehearsal and found it was actually happening.

JK: Did it surprise you that the band had decided to carry on with another singer? There was certainly a huge outpouring of opinion from the fans on the subject.

OW: I think because they had done it in the past with Trevor Horn and set the precedent with him, I kind of thought they might do it again at some point. As to the mind-set of the members of the band and how they did that, I think that is part of the internal conflicts that have gone on within the band since day one. There's always an element of a power struggle going on within Yes, and I think it was just that element playing itself out in a certain way. From my personal point of view, I was disappointed that I didn't get to work with Jon, although we had exchanged musical ideas with each other. Jon was determined that he wanted the band to do new songs on the tour, and he sent me some of these songs. I had written some piano parts for the songs, and he was keen to do an album as well, but then he got ill, and everything stopped, which was a shame. He was putting together this whole new project for Yes, which for me would have been a great introduction to the band, as people would have heard me on an album before I toured with the band. I was also disappointed not to work with Jon on stage as well, although I did make a great friend with Benoit for two reasons, really. One: we were both new boys that joined at the same time, and we were learning as we went along, and two: we just really got on well with each other and still do, in fact.

JK: Going back to that first rehearsal that you were so happy to be part of, can you remember the first song that you played with the band?

OW: Yeah, "Owner Of A Lonely Heart." I think it was because Steve said it was the easiest.

JK: That is funny because Steve has always said he was not a great lover of that song. Although, in recent years, he has had to play it a lot and may have got used to it.

OW: Yeah, I don't think Steve is ever going to be overly keen on the Trevor

Rabin era of the band. I think it is normal that people don't like the idea that a band can be more successful without them. I think that is understandable because he wasn't part of the band then, but he can take solace in the fact that he was responsible for a lot of the music that is revered historically.

JK: What was the first show like, then? Sometimes you can be so hyped up that you get through it without making any mistakes, purely in adrenaline, but the subsequent shows, when your guard is down, is where the mistakes happen.

OW: Well, during the first four shows everyone made some mistakes, and there were a few things that went awry, although nothing dreadful. There were a couple of moments when everyone wasn't quite sure where they were because Yes music, as opposed to being straight 4/4, there are lots of times where you are counting 16, and then you are waiting for three bars, and then only playing two notes. There's a lot of that kind of stuff, and it's only with the familiarity of playing with people time and time again that you get used to their cues and their way of playing and how everybody reacts onstage with each other. These are the things that make Yes sound particularly amazing, and when all those things kick in and work, that is when it becomes quite special. Yes is not a jam band, by any stretch of the imagination. You can't just get up and bluff your way through it. I had all sorts of pieces of paper with notes on them, but after show five, it started to all come together.

It was an enjoyable time, though. I think I was away for about ten weeks, including that initial two-week rehearsal. It's like any new job, really. The first few weeks are when you are trying to find your feet and find out what you are doing. But it became relaxed pretty quickly, and we started to enjoy it as we became better at it.

JK: Did you get a better appreciation of what your Dad went through, both performing and even writing this kind of music? As you say, you can't just get up and bluff it. There is a lot of thought that has gone into it.

OW: There is, but then again, he went into it and created some of the more challenging aspects of it by helping to create songs like "Heart Of The Sunrise," "Close To The Edge," and "Siberian Khatru." They were the pieces that were tricky, and I mean particularly tricky. There were elements of trickiness on *The Yes Album* as well with things like "Perpetual Change" and "Yours Is No Disgrace," which have elements of difficulty. I have immense respect for anyone who has been in Yes, from a musician's point of view. The tour manager said to me, "You're doing really well. Remember, there are only a few musicians on the planet that can play this stuff." That made me feel quite good and think, *Well, I'm doing alright.*

The hardest thing was when I decided to go down this authenticity route. The band were keen on that too, but they didn't want to play the songs as they did on the album. They wanted the parts to be played like the album, but the arrangements to be the live arrangements. For example, with "Roundabout," they wanted the same sounds as on the record, but they wanted to re-arrange the middle section slightly. Or, they would want to do "Yours Is No Disgrace" with all the Moog parts and the harmony parts on the organ that hadn't been played for years, but then do this vamping part in the middle. I would ask Chris how many times he played that, and he would say, "I think it's four." So every night I would play four, and it would be wrong. So I asked the guy doing the sound to make me tapes so could listen to the band. I would then find that it wasn't four but six, and when I told Chris that, Chris would say, "Oh, I thought it was four," and he had been naturally playing it that way for years. So in effect, I could never just sit down at home and practice along with the record, because the arrangement wouldn't be right. And I couldn't sit down and play along to the live recording, because the parts wouldn't be right. It was only when you were up there playing and putting all the bits together that you could see how it went. It was challenging, but that was the fun and the satisfaction of when it all went right.

JK: You say that you wanted to bring authenticity to the band, and there were two tracks that I was pleased that the band chose to perform, "Tempus Fugit" and "Machine Messiah," both from the *Drama* album. The band could never perform them with Jon, so how did you approach those?

OW: The same way I approached all the songs. I just sat down and worked them all out and learned them. I felt they deserved the same level of detail as the other songs in the set and the songs that Dad had played on. In fact, I think everyone thought the set was going to be based around an awful lot of stuff Dad had played, but I was playing across the board in terms of material. I was playing stuff that Patrick Moraz, Tony Kaye, and Geoff Downes had played; even stuff that Trevor Rabin had played. When Jon was in the band, he was talking about playing songs from *The Ladder*, so that would have meant me playing songs that Igor and Billy Sherwood had played on. So, as I said when Dad joined, he was playing them his own way and adapting and amending things, whereas I was adapting my playing to match everybody else's style of playing.

JK: I suppose the advantage of those two songs was that Chris, Alan, and Steve had not played those songs since the *Drama* tour.

OW: No. That was quite encouraging to see them with big sheets in front of them with notes, although Chris does have an incredible memory. For example, when we were playing "Siberian Khatru" he said, "Can you play the main riff when we get to the minor section?" and I said, "But it's not on the record, Chris," and he said, "It is," so I said, "No, that is not on the record." We listened to it, and then he said, "Oh, well, I think your Dad was playing that in the studio when we were rehearsing it, so can you play it?" (*Laughs*) I said, "Chris, I wasn't born then when you recorded it!" And he said, "Well, can you work out what your Dad would have done then?" So I had to take this riff, which was in seconds and fourths, which is not a normal keyboard riff and work it in. Chris listened to it and said, "Yeah, that'll do it." So, Chris would never really have that problem. You would just say, "Let's do 'Tempus Fugit,'" and Chris would say, "Okay," and be there.

JK: Well, over the years, with regards to "Tempus Fugit," Chris has used that main riff as part of his bass solo, but for me, "Tempus Fugit" and "Machine Messiah" are huge pieces of Yes music.

OW: Well, they are, but they are a different style of writing to the likes of, say, "Close To The Edge." As I was saying before, with the counting in "Close To the Edge," there are like five lines of music intertwining. "Machine Messiah" from a song construction point is a lot more simplistic in that it is like eight pieces bolted together and you can see where the joints are. Whereas, with "Close To The Edge" or "Siberian Khatru," the joints are a lot less defined. I think part of that is the way Geoff Downes plays, which is very good for the kind of stuff that he plays with Asia. That is not a criticism, but with John Wetton, he has also found someone who plays with that style very well. That doesn't make "Machine Messiah" any less important as a piece of music. However, it is definitely a different style compared to "Close To The Edge," which is a strange song. In that one minute, you can be playing the main part, and then the next you are into the "I Get Down" part, and you wonder, *How did I get here?*

JK: Once you got into the touring cycle, you made some of the shows available on memory stick to purchase after the concert. I have listened to some of them and compared them to the *Live In Lyon* album, and you are very consistent as a band on the various performances.

OW: Well, that was 2009, and that was the tour around Europe. We had toured America in autumn 2008, and we had done a gig in the spring. Then Chris got ill, and after that, we had done the tour with Asia. So, as a band, we had got into the mindset that we had been together for a year, and we started to talk about doing an album. Well, Chris and I were very keen to do an album, and we were really pushing for it. And as they knew I wrote a lot, I think they thought I would be a good addition to the band, in that sense. So it was on that tour that we discussed that, but also on that tour USB recording came up in conversation, and I said, "I know a guy in the UK who has a studio. Since we have recorded about eight shows, why don't you give me the hard disc and I'll go and put together a live album?" And that is what happened because I thought those shows were really good and deserving of release.

In fact, we also filmed two shows for the live album, but the show the first night was not as good because we had travelled into France after about five days of gigs the length and breadth of the UK. The first show in France was not as good as the second show, so I went into the studio thinking I only have the one show that is any good. Any bits I had to fix I could do so from other shows because I really wanted it to be a good representation of what people were coming to the shows for. I didn't want to get into the thing of bringing people in to overdub, because, on previous Yes DVDs, I had noticed that sometimes the fingers weren't anywhere near where they should be. I suppose many people do think of live albums as stop gaps, or not as important as studio albums, or the record company wants a live album to put out. But I was very aware that it had to be good. I also felt that as Jon and Dad weren't in the band, I wanted it to be a good album that proved that the band was great and still worth coming to see.

JK: Listening to one of the shows on USB and the live album, it is very hard to choose because the band were very consistent at this time. I think the live shows proved that the band had validity and were worth coming to see in a live situation.

OW: Yeah, and also from a personal point of view, I wanted to make sure all the instruments were equally balanced. Sometimes, depending on where you sit in an auditorium, you don't always get the balance. Sometimes the keyboards or the vocals are too quiet, and the only way of hearing everything properly is through a live album. I wanted to make it sound good from that respect, and from a personal point of view, it was nice to get the opportunity to work on a live product.

JK: We have to talk about the studio album that you started but unfortunately didn't finish. You are credited as a co-writer on "Into The Storm," and also credited as a player on the album. You say yourself and Chris were very keen on the album, but how did everyone else in the band feel? Did they feel the same way, or did the need to be convinced?

OW: Well, there were a couple who needed to be convinced. Benoit didn't really write music, but he was happy to go along with it. Steve was putting out albums with Asia, and obviously his solo albums, so he felt if we did an album it had to be a really good album, and he was adamant that it would be me and him doing the production and putting it together.

We started putting it together in Phoenix in the March of 2010, and I became the engineer. We had this laptop, and we had songs that I had written, songs Steve had written, songs that Chris had written, and there was a song that Chris and I had written. There were also pieces of music from Steve that I had arranged, and then stuff that Steve and I had written at Steve's house in Devon. There was this lovely integration of Chris, Steve, and myself writing and putting stuff together. We had a fair bit of music together at the time, and then we went on tour for the summer. When we got back, the subject of production came up. Steve wanted me and him to do it, but Chris wasn't keen on being produced, as he wanted to have some involvement himself, which I didn't mind. I was happy for that to happen. Benoit, on the other hand, wasn't sure that we should be producing ourselves. So at that point, I suggested that they try and get Trevor Horn involved because it would have been a nice touch. With Jon and Dad not being in the band, they could take something from a time when Jon was in the band, and it would give the album some validity.

Then Steve said that the band had to feel like a band, both onstage and off, before we could record anything. We had to be a band because any album that came out of that would have to be representative of the band. So, we started the album proper in Los Angeles at the end of that year, and it was going well. There was some good music going around. Trevor Horn came in from the start and was listening to a lot of the material we were doing, and he liked it. He picked out a piece of my music, which he particularly liked; so everything was going fine, and then all of a sudden, he wanted to do a piece of music that turned out to be the song "Fly From Here." I asked why we should be doing this old song, and Trevor said, "Well, we recorded it in 1980 and it was never on the album, and I remember thinking to myself, *Well, it's been on the boxed set and also on a Buggles album, so why are we doing it now to showcase a new line-up of the band on a new album?* It didn't seem to make much sense to me, to be honest, particularly as we had such camaraderie as a five-piece. I said we should stand or fall by what we wrote together.

So, as we went along, Trevor got more into this piece. He would say, "I can't remember how this piece went," and so he would write to Geoff and Geoff would send the keyboard part back, and Trevor would work on other pieces.

When I was meant to fly back after Christmas, it got to the point where I didn't get invited back. I was due to fly out, and I got delayed, and then I got delayed again, and I was told, "Oh, Trevor just wants to do one more track." Then he wanted Geoff to fly out and work on a track. So, suddenly, Geoff was in the studio, and I wasn't. I think what it boiled down to was that he just wanted to work with Geoff. He was comfortable working with Geoff and writing with Geoff. I think the other guys in Yes wanted Trevor, and if they wanted Trevor, they had to have Geoff, and I think that is really how it came about.

JK: With regards to the material that you wrote, there is only one song bearing your credit as a co-writer. What happened to all the other material you were working on? Would you like to see it come out at some point, perhaps with your own band?

OW: Well, I am working on two albums at the moment, which I hope will come out; one this year [2012] and one next year. One of them is a solo album that I have recorded with my band, and I have re-recorded two or three of the songs for that. The other album is an album with Gordon Giltrap called *Ravens and Lullabies*. What happened was, I got the songs back from America and removed the other guys' parts. I re-recorded them, as I didn't want to use their parts. My band recorded the parts we wiped, and that will come out as an album called *Cultural Vandalism*. The remaining songs are for the album I have recorded with Gordon Giltrap. So, I have made use of the music; it wasn't going to go to waste.

JK: So you are off the album, but you had to go back and play some live dates with the band. Geoff had commitments with Asia and wasn't able to tour with Yes at that point. So, you had to go back and play some dates on the tour in the run-up to the album coming out.

OW: Well, once I was out of the band, there were a couple of points of view. One: if the album wasn't coming out until the summer, it made sense for Geoff to re-join then. Plus, the tour had already been advertised. And two: two nobody knew I wasn't in the band at this point because they hadn't announced it. So, we had one day's rehearsal before the tour, and that was pretty awkward; it has to be said. It was a very difficult period, but at the end of the day, I looked at it as "I am a professional musician. I'll just treat it as a session. I'm out on tour, and this band is paying me to play this music, and people are buying tickets and coming to see the show. I'll do the best that I can," which is what I try and do with every show I do, even though it was incredibly difficult. And of course, I had a wife and family to support back home. I also didn't want to be one of those people who gets into a big slagging match in the press; it just didn't appeal to me.

JK: I think that is absolutely the right way to look at it. If we look back over the whole period of time you were in the band, your part in the whole Yes jigsaw was actually a very important part because you provided the bridge for the band to continue in many ways.

OW: Yeah, and it was actually while we were on that tour that there were some rumblings from within the band that maybe they had made the wrong decision. I think when we started playing, and like you say in 2009, when we were playing we were like a well-oiled machine, and two years down the line we were even tighter. For example, Chris and Steve would say, "Hey, let's do 'Perpetual Change,'" and we could get up and play it after one practice run-through. They would go, "Yeah, that's pretty good!" It was that kind of level of competence in that we all knew how we played and interacted with each other. The eye contact with each other onstage was good. We knew what to listen for, and we could put together pieces like "Perpetual Change" relatively quickly, which I think was a great example of just how well the band was working at that point.

I don't ever claim that the line-up I was in would have any level of immortality that, say, the version with Dad or the version with Bill in the band would have. Those days were very important days for the band with mass markets and unlimited other media distractions. But I still think it was an important period of the band's history; it showed that they could keep going without some of the major members.

JK: Apart from the way it ended, perhaps, can you look back on your time in the band and say, "Yeah, I did a good job there"?

OW: Oh, yeah. I am very proud of the time I spent in the band. The nicest thing I think I read was on a forum, and I know you shouldn't really delve into forums, but sometimes you can't help coming across stuff. This guy had posted something on YouTube, and this guy was having a real pop at me, you know, a real go. And those sort of things you do find a little upsetting when you are trying to do your best. But then I went onto another forum when the *Live In Lyon* album came out, and this same guy had started a post on there, and it went along the lines of, "I've just heard this *Live In Lyon* album, and I'd like to take back everything bad I've said about Oliver Wakeman. Now I can hear the mix; I can hear what this guy was doing."

I thought that, A) That was really nice for me to hear because it meant that I could be appreciated for what I tried to do through a live album, and B) That it was good for the fans that were able to listen to something musically, and realise that people aren't as blinkered as they sometimes say they are, and are able to say, "Actually, that mix was bad, and I couldn't hear what was going on, but now I can hear, and I get it, and this is actually pretty cool." So, it is a period of my life that I can look back on with a certain amount of fondness, but I also feel it never came to its proper conclusion. I never felt that that line-up had its chance to show what it could really do. Technically I was with the band from January 2008 until July 2011, so I was in there a long time, really, in the scheme of things; just over three and a half years on paper.

JK: You were actually a member longer, I think, than Patrick Moraz and Geoff Downes in his first stint with the band.

OW: Yeah, I was in there longer than a few members of the band; Igor as well, I think.

JK: I think you may have just beaten your Dad's first period in the band as well, time-wise.

OW: I think it may have been because I also know with the band I played over 150 shows, so I did a fair amount of playing. Even though on record I did just the one live album and played on part of the studio album, my actual tenure in the band was quite a lengthy one, so I am proud of that. And I am proud of the fact that I did it because it was quite a high-pressured job to take on; it taught me a lot of things. It taught me musically, it taught me things about international touring, and it also taught me a lot about the different personalities of the calibre of musician I was playing within Yes. Even though it didn't end the way I would have liked it to have ended, it gave me the drive to continue doing this as a career, which, of course, is what I continue to do now.

Oliver has continued to record and play concerts, with the most recent tour being the Oliver Wakeman Gordon Giltrap tour of the UK. Both the albums that feature music that Oliver wrote while with Yes are scheduled to be released in the first half of 2013, with the *Ravens And Lullabies* album scheduled for release first.

≈

Phil Franks: Shooting The Yes Album Sleeve
November 2012

Phil Franks was heavily involved in the burgeoning Ladbroke Grove scene in the late 60s and early 70s. He was responsible for many iconic images in both the underground press like Friends Magazine and the mainstream press like Rolling Stone Magazine. He also became involved with many great album sleeves, including sleeves for Quiver (*Gone In The Morning*), Frank Zappa (*Chunga's Revenge*), and Hawkwind (*In Search Of Space*). And, of course, he was the photographer on the sessions for *The Yes Album*.

The Yes Album **was a very important album for Yes. It was their third album and also their first hit album, making the Top 10 on its release in early 1971. The cover that is now universally known as the sleeve for *The Yes Album*, however, was not the original concept, as Phil Franks explains in this interview.**

Jon Kirkman (JK): First of all, Phil, let's set up the background as to how you came to be in London and involved in the cover for *The Yes Album*. You did a lot of work for Friends Magazine, which was based in London and was an "underground" publication. So how did you come to work for that organisation?

Phil Franks (PF): Well, I'd moved into a flat in Portobello Road just up the road from where the Friends Magazine office was, and I had always been interested in photography from when I was a kid. I had recently bought a camera and was walking down Portobello Road one day, and I ran into a guy called Pat Mescal…well, that is what he was called back then! (*Laughs*) He saw my camera and asked me if I knew how to use it and if I knew how to do darkroom work, which is basically knowing how to print and develop your own pictures. So I told him I did because I had learnt that at the youth club I used to attend. So, to cut a long story short, he told me he was working for a guy called Eric Hayes who, at the time, was doing all the London work for Rolling Stone Magazine and a helluva lot of work for record companies and was responsible for a lot of well-known album sleeves back then.

So, Pat was working in this dark room that he had built in the basement of the property next to the offices of Friends Magazine, which happened to be Barney Bubbles' studio and house. So that is basically how I got into working in photography in that late 60s early 70s scene. I was working down in this basement printing and developing stuff for Eric Hayes alongside this guy Pat Mescal. Since Eric wasn't interested in doing anything for Friends Magazine, and I was handy, and they were next door, I did stuff for them if they needed anything done.

When Eric went back to Canada (where he was originally from), I inherited a lot of his work for Rolling Stone Magazine in London, although most of my work was still for Friends Magazine, which was next door. There was also a lot of stuff for Barney Bubbles as well. For instance, the work I did for Hawkwind, including the photographs on the *In Search Of Space* album sleeve, was through Barney, and also some sleeves I did for Quiver.

JK: I know Quiver were on Warner Brothers, and Warner Bros. and Atlantic were together as labels. Was there any connection between doing the sleeve for the Quiver album and you getting the job for *The Yes Album*, as Yes were on Atlantic?

PF: No, there was no connection; that would be just coincidental. I just knew the boys in Quiver because they lived near to me and we would often drop into each other's place. So we were socialising a lot, as it was that kind of a situation, but most of the work that I did for Barney came about through knowing the bands, rather than the record companies, in those days. So I was always bumping into those kinds of people like Hawkwind and Quiver on Portobello Road.

The guy that was responsible for the Yes sleeve was a guy called John Goodchild, who had been away for a while working for Rolling Stone in San Francisco. He came back and did a kind of "Guest Art Directorship" of Friends Magazine, so that is how I met him. And he knew Barney and the work I had done for Barney and Friends Magazine, so that is the connection there for the Yes sleeve. He asked me if I would be interested in doing the photography for that sleeve for him, as he was the art director on that sleeve. He was what you would call a "serious art director." Back then, it was all a bit of a game, and everyone was trying to push the envelope a bit. It was a time of new ideas and traditions being thrown out of the window. But the thing that Barney, John, and I had in common, which of course, others shared as well, was a love of good work and doing a professional job in the classic sense. I always aimed to be a good photographer. I put a lot of importance on getting a good black and white negative correctly developed and getting a technically good print from those negatives.

JK: I believe you prefer to work in black and white. Why is that?

PF: Yeah, I do prefer black and white, and to be honest, I didn't find colour as easy to manage. Maybe it is because I came from the background of working in a dark room and developing my own photographs back at the youth club in Hackney, where I grew up as a kid. I don't know. But I did work for a while with a guy developing colour slides. It is a whole different kettle of fish, and I never really mastered it. It is much more complicated. So for that reason, black and white is simpler to work with, and I also prefer the results, if I'm honest with you. There are some photographers that are great at using colour in their photography, but I prefer the light, the shade, and the highlights of black and white.

JK: There are three distinct photo sessions for *The Yes Album*, and none of them are in black and white, are they?

PF: Well, I did occasionally shoot in colour when I was commissioned to, so I always had some rolls of colour film with me if I was asked.

JK Of the three sessions, (which were Advision Studios, the soundcheck at the Lyceum, and your flat), which one was used for the actual cover, and which of the sessions came first?

PF: I think it was Advision Studios where the band were recording the album first, and then the Lyceum, if I remember correctly, and finally my flat. Have you seen the cover of the reissued album?

JK: Yes, I have. I have that album.

PF: Well, the picture of the plastic head burning was my favourite photo of the session, and I suggested that to John Goodchild and said, "I think that should be the cover," and he got back to me and said, "The band didn't like it." I didn't actually have a relationship with the band, and I don't mean that in a negative way. Both at Advision and the Lyceum, they were totally into doing their thing, recording and getting ready to do a concert, and I was totally into taking photos of them and being unobtrusive. I wasn't one of those photographers that used to get in there and say, "I want you to do this or do that." There was an unwritten rule that you really didn't do that. So that is kind of how I approached the session at Advision and also at the Lyceum; not to get in their way.

JK: The original concept for the cover of the album was not the cover that eventually came out though, was it?

PF: No, not at all. John Goodchild had this idea, and we had actually done some black and white test shots of it in a studio. I think I still have them somewhere. Basically, they are of the backs of some Marshall stacks with "Yes" stencilled across the backs of the speaker cabinets. Anyway, we were working to John's idea, which was to have the bandstand in front of these cabinets, and this was probably the only time I had worked with an art director who said basically, "This is what I want you to shoot." So, we managed to get this all set up with the Hasselblad camera, and the amps set up, and the flash set up, while we waited for the band to turn up. But when the band turned up a little later than we thought, we couldn't get the bloody stuff to work. The flash would just not work, even though we tried for a while to get it working, it just wouldn't work. Time was slipping by, and due to the fact that the band had been in a crash, I think the day before or a couple of days before the session, (hence the plaster on Tony Kaye's leg), and the band's lateness due to Tony going to the hospital, we were running out of time, because the band had to get off and do another gig that evening.

So, with time getting on, I suggested to John that we go back to my place and shoot the band there. I had photographed plenty of other people there, so I was used to working there. I just used to put the 1000 watt bulb in the light holder and off we went. We went there in a cab, and outside the flat, I saw this plastic head, either in a skip or in the road, I can't remember, but I picked it up and thought, *I can use that*.

JK: How many pictures did you manage to take during the session in the kitchen?

PF: Well, it would be just that one roll of infra-red film. I had bought this film, and I had used a couple of other rolls before and experimented with it, and I just thought, *Let's use this and see what we get*. And when I suggested that to John Goodchild, he just said, "Yeah, do whatever you like." They wanted something in colour, as the photos at Advision and the Lyceum had been. But rather than use Kodachrome or Ektachrome film, I decided to use this weird stuff.

JK: Well it obviously worked because the album sleeve has become an iconic image now. And of course, it was the band's first hit album, and it made the Top 10, so millions of people worldwide recognise that sleeve.

PF: Oh, it is a great album! I love it, and I still listen to it a lot. I remember hearing the band record parts of "Starship Trooper" when I was photographing them in Advision.

JK: Did you get sent a copy of the album when it was finished?

PF: Actually, not always by the record company. As I have said, most of the work I did was either directly with the bands, or through Barney Bubbles, or in this instance, John Goodchild. And he saw to it that I got a copy of the album when it was released.

JK: When you look at it now, do you like it and think it turned out okay? Or do you prefer your original idea, which the band didn't like, with the polystyrene head on fire and the flames dripping off the head? Can you live with the image that was chosen?

PF: Oh yeah, that's fine. That was the image that was chosen by John Goodchild and the band. He was the one who had a relationship with the band and the record company. My only connection with the band was that I was photographing them. John Goodchild was the art director on the sleeve, and I dealt directly with him. He asked me how much I wanted to get paid for the job, and I told him, and he made sure I got it. So he dealt with all the business side of it, really. I'm not sure whether it was the band or the record company that didn't like that shot I suggested for the cover, with the dripping plastic on fire. My memory is that the band didn't like it, but it was such a long time ago! (*Laughs*)

I think the cover works quite well. They are all grouped together in a corner with a strange head floating with one of them sitting down. And then on the back of the sleeve, they've all gone, and the head is just there floating above the chair.

JK: I think 40+ years on as an album it still stands up musically, and also the artwork is still very striking, particularly knowing that it came out of something that was almost made up on the spot.

PF: Well, that's right, although nobody except John Goodchild and I knew that! (*Laughs*) I'm glad it turned out well, but that is down to John Goodchild making the best of my photos, really. If I am honest, they weren't the best photos I had taken, as far as photos go, partly as I said, I didn't particularly like working with colour. It was also difficult to get the colours right, which is why at the end I just threw my arms up in the air and said, "Fuck it. I'll use infra-red, which will fuck the colours up even more."

JK: So you just made it look like it was deliberate, then?

PF: (*Laughs*) Yeah, that's right! I always took pride in getting nice, crisp, black and white photographs, and that didn't happen with the Yes cover! The colour stuff was all off in Advision. There is one of Chris Squire where he looks all green. I couldn't get the lighting right with the fluorescent tube lighting. And at the Lyceum, the stage lighting caused problems. Stage lighting anywhere is notoriously over-saturated. It looks good on stage, but it isn't good for taking photos with because stage lighting is all blues and reds and strong tones.

The thing about the infra-red film as well is that the actual infra-red rays that the film is recording are not the visible light you see, so it looks slightly out of focus. There is a trick – you have to focus slightly in front of the subject to get infra-red shots in focus, so in that sense, I was slightly disappointed.

JK: Well, even though you personally don't think they were the best photographs you ever took, here we are, 42 years later, still talking about them.

PF: Well, artistically, they worked. And again, I say that is all merit to John Goodchild. He was another brilliant art director like Barney Bubbles, and he used a lot of my work, including some stuff that I had not shot for that purpose. But he had the eye for something and thought, *Well, I can use that for something*, and John Goodchild was the same, which is why *The Yes Album* sleeve turned out so well.

Phil Franks now lives in Spain. He oversees his archive and is responsible for the website: The Philm Freaks Digital Archive. You can check out Phil's work (including outtakes from *The Yes Album* sessions) at the website here:

http://www.ibiblio.org/mal/MO/philm/index.html

~

Tony Kaye: From Yes To Circa And Back To Yes
April 2012

Tony Kaye was a founding member of Yes and was the keyboard player on the band's first three albums. This included the band's first successful chart album in the UK, *The Yes Album*. Following his time with Yes, Tony played a session for former Yes bandmate Peter Banks on the debut album of Peter's new band Flash. While this was happening, Tony was also forming a band with another Yes-related musician, David Foster. David was the bassist with Jon Anderson's first group The Warriors.

Badger decided to record their debut album in a live situation, and the ideal opportunity came about when the band supported Yes at the Rainbow Theatre in London with Jon Anderson producing. Badger would make a second album in 1974 with a totally different line-up and had moved into a totally different genre of music. From Badger, Tony found himself with Michael des Barres in Detective. Detective recorded and released two albums for Led Zeppelin's Swan Song Records label before folding in the late 70s. From here, Tony became the keyboard player in the reformed Badfinger alongside Joey Molland and Tommy Evans.

After touring and recording with Badfinger, Tony heard once more from Chris Squire, who was then working on a project with Alan White and Trevor Rabin. This project would become Cinema and subsequently Yes. Tony Kaye agreed to take us through the twists and turns in an exclusive interview in April 2012. We started off by discussing *The Yes Album*.

Jon Kirkman (JK): While I was looking through some photos from the sessions for the cover of *The Yes Album*, I read a story about how your leg came to be in plaster. It's an amazing story! I have had the album for years and always wondered why your leg or foot was in plaster.

Tony Kaye (TK): (*Laughs*) Yes well, that was when we were coming back from a gig in Devon I think, Barnstaple or somewhere down there, and it was pissing with rain on the way back. It was late, about one or two o'clock in the morning, and it was meant to be a freeway. Chris was driving, Jon, Peter, and Bill were in the back, and I was in the passenger seat. We thought it was just a regular motorway, and actually the other lanes had been closed. I don't exactly remember which road it was, or why it was like that, but it turned out to be closed. It was just two lanes and we were overtaking a truck and we hit head-on into another car coming in the opposite direction.

JK: That doesn't sound good.

TK: No, no. It was not good, and the impact shoved the engine through the front compartment partially and it hit my foot!

JK: I suppose the photo session next day for the cover must have been pretty low down on your list of priorities.

TK: Yeah, it was. Actually, I don't think it was the next day because I went to the hospital and it wasn't that apparent that it was broken. But I woke up the next morning and my foot was huge, so I had to go to the hospital the next day to get a cast put on it, so I think it was somewhat later that the photo was taken.

JK: Well, it's a striking cover, even with the plaster cast on!

TK: (*Laughs*) Yeah!

JK: So, what were those three years with Yes like? Having spoken to Chris Squire about the album, the reason *The Yes Album* became so popular was almost a fluke. There was a postal strike on and they had to get the chart returns from different shops, I think it was the Virgin record shops, and *The Yes Album* was selling very well in those shops.

TK: Oh, well, that's a good story. I wasn't aware of that.

JK: Well, I think it was well-known at the time, and I heard it confirmed from Chris Squire. In the three years, you were in the band. There were the first two albums and then the line-up changed, and Steve Howe was brought into the band for *The Yes Album*. Was it a big surprise when you were asked to leave or sacked? I'm not really sure that anyone actually leaves Yes. It is a bit like the Secret Service – you can't retire!

TK: Yes, it is a bit like that. But, you know, back then you're young… (*laughs*) you have no fear, and we had just returned from our first tour of the States. We toured the States with Jethro Tull, Alice Cooper, and a few other people, and we were just really beginning to sort of get recognition. I must admit, I loved the States, and I got a little rock n roll. I was probably the "Bad Boy" in the band, and I was really not conforming to the idea of what was a serious band, as you might well imagine.

JK: That's a very diplomatic answer.

TK: It was serious music that was seriously played with personalities, mainly

Steve... (*laughs*) that was quite serious, and I was a bit of a loose cannon, actually. Even though we had spent three years putting this music together, which was unlike anything else, really, that was going on. I was a more bluesy kind of guy, and I had discovered North American bands that I loved, like The Band; they were my favourites! And I loved Southern blues and rock. I was generally digging American music, and the music we were making really had none of those elements at all. Yes was not influenced by any blues at all. It was a little strange for me. I wanted to rock out a little more, and I was primarily a Hammond player, playing extremely loud Hammond. In fact, as loud as I could make it, and with somewhat of a blues influence – and Peter Banks was too.

JK: Is that why you decided to play on the first Flash album, then? It was around the same time as Badger, and I can see the lineage between Yes into Flash and into Badger.

TK: Well, you know, Peter kind of kept that Yes thing alive in what he did with Flash. It was very, very Yes influenced, but I had nothing to do with that band. I left Yes, and I already had a band with David Foster and Brian Parrish (Badger). We already had that together, and that was MY band. In fact, it was a side project before I left Yes. But because Peter and I had remained friends, I played on the Flash album, but I was never going to join the band. I was too busy doing Badger at that time.

So Yes did another American tour and came back to the UK. They were going to do a live gig at The Rainbow, but they had all their gear impounded as they came back into the UK. So, Jon rang me and asked if the band could come down to our rehearsal space and use our gear to rehearse for this gig at the Rainbow, as their gig was impounded at Heathrow. So they came down, we vacated the rehearsal studio, and they rehearsed. To back up a little, we had only rehearsed a little while; it wasn't like we had rehearsed for weeks and weeks. So, during this period, Jon said, "Why don't you support Yes at the Rainbow? And as we are recording it, why don't you record it?" So that's what happened.

JK: Well, the first Badger album came out, and then there was a change not only with the line-up but also with the music on *White Lady*. You brought in Jackie Lomax, and it was a completely different sound, although he is a great singer.

TK: Yeah, but even though I wanted a more Southern blues influence, that really took over. You know, I love Jackie, and he had a great voice. And of course, Kim Gardener and Roy Dyke were in there, but it changed the band.

Then we got a deal with what was CBS or Epic, and decided to go to New Orleans with Allen Toussaint producing, for Christ sake! (*Laughs*)

JK: Well, it was almost a 180-degree turn from the first album.

TK: Yes, very much so. I thought it would be a sort of turn, but it didn't quite turn out to what it should have been. It was very cool to go to New Orleans, and Alan Toussaint is an amazing artist, but it was a little too different from the little old Badger! (*Laughs*)

JK: Well, let's move on again. You were in two other bands in the 70s that people would remember. You were in Detective with Michael des Barres, and then Badfinger. In the 80s you were involved with Yes again, but there was a band before that called Cinema. Were you actually involved with Cinema?

TK: Yeah, with regards to Detective, I had been on tour for two years with David Bowie. I did the *Thin White Duke* Tour. I got back kind of crazy because it was a crazy time and a crazy tour. I got back to LA and bumped into Michael, who had been in Silverhead, who had just put together Detective. And of course, that was destined to do big things. We were with Swan Song, and Led Zeppelin used to come and see us. We also did a tour with Kiss.

JK: Can I ask you something here? Perhaps you can confirm or deny an urban myth here. Did Jimmy Page produce the first Detective album under a pseudonym?

TK: No, no. We were just with Swan Song, and that was it. We were really a local band here in LA, and we used to play at a club called The Starwood. We played there quite a lot, and the whole band would come down and see us with Peter Grant. But no, other than that, they didn't have anything to do with recording the band.

JK: That's the urban myth, you see, and with the Internet these stories become true.

TK: Oh, yeah. I had heard it, and it's not true, but that thing kind of fizzled out. Of course, it was obviously very Led Zeppelin influenced, and I had a kind of hard job trying to fit Hammond and keyboards into the band, so it was a little bit strange for me. So then I bumped into Tommy and Joey one day, and they had just put Badfinger back together and recorded *Airwaves*. They asked me to join the band, and I recruited a couple of people I had been working with. I brought them into the band, like the drummer and the guitar player Glen. We decided to go down to Miami to record a new

Badfinger album, and just by chance, we were living next door to Chris' wife and kids. So Yes came to town, the Yes with Trevor Horn and Geoff Downes; I think it was the *Drama* tour. So we went to the show, hung out, and then we all went back and partied at Nikki's holiday villa. So after a while, Chris and I started talking along the lines of how it's going, what's the thing about Jon, how's Trevor Horn working out, etc., and he said, "Yeah, it's okay, but I'd really like to do something different."

Of course, he went back, and Alan and Chris started working with Jimmy Page in XYZ. During that time, I was still here doing the Badfinger album in Miami, which lasted about nine months, I think. It took a long time, and Chris had bumped into Trevor Rabin in London, who was auditioning for Asia. So those two got together, and then Trevor was living here in Los Angeles. He came back and called me, and we got together. Then Chris called, and Trevor and I went back over there. It was nothing to do with Yes; it was Trevor, Chris, Alan, and myself. That was how Cinema began, and that was when it started.

JK: So, when exactly did Jon come back into the picture?

TK: Well, we rehearsed for nine months, and then we went into the studio with Trevor Horn and recorded *90125*, or what became *90125*. That was the Cinema album, which Atlantic had picked up and was going to release as Cinema. Jon came over to the studio one day from Paris, heard the album and freaked! He said, "I really want to sing on this!" The album was actually complete with Trevor Rabin singing, but once the powers that be (the management and the record company) heard this, they were only too happy to let that happen because they saw dollars and they saw Yes! So, Jon came into the studio and re-did the vocals, and we became Yes…and subsequently huge!

JK: I can remember being absolutely stunned when I heard the album because I liked the *Drama* album, and I know a lot of people did not like that album. It was a very contentious period for the band, sadly, because I thought *Drama* was really good. But then they split, and Asia came along, I thought that was it, as far as Yes were concerned. Jon seemed very happy and established in his solo career, but all of a sudden it's Yes again! And not only that, you are back in the band! That surprised me because there was the talk of Eddie Jobson being in the band; I think Eddie is in the video for "Owner Of A Lonely Heart."

TK: Yeah, "Owner Of A Lonely Heart." I had actually left the band. I'd had enough in London. I was sick of London, and I was sick of the band… (*laughs*) so I quit the band. I was booked to do a tour with Badfinger anyway.

So I came back to do the tour, and then Tommy died, so that didn't happen, and I was just back in LA hanging about. I had no idea what was going on with the band.

Do you know what Swap Meets are? Well, I had set up a t-shirt business (*laughs*) just to make some money. I used to go to these Swap Meets to sell these t-shirts, all sorts of things, you know; rock n roll t-shirts and TV Icon t-shirts, just making money. I was at a Swap Meet selling t-shirts, and I had my Ghetto Blaster with me, and I heard this song and thought, *That sounds familiar…* and it was "Owner Of A Lonely Heart." And about a week after that, Trevor called me and said, "We're going on tour, are you in?"

JK: And that phone call set you off on another two or three years-worth of touring off the back of that album.

TK: Yeah, that was a long, long tour.

JK: Why did it take so long after that tour to get *Big Generator* together? It seemed to take forever. It didn't come out until 1987, which, at the time, was a long time. Not considered too long these days, but back then it was a long time between records. If you didn't bring another album out quickly, people would forget, wouldn't they?

TK: Yeah, I know. You know Jon, it was a combination of a lot of things. Being on the road that length of time was a pretty heavy deal constantly. You're constantly playing, and really no one was writing anything. We were working, partying, playing, and having a good time. And of course, the album was so successful that it just went on and on. We toured the world a couple of times and so time went by. Suddenly we realised how much time had gone by and that we needed to make a new album. But we had to start right from the beginning because no one had material. So, we rented a house here in the Hollywood Hills and started writing, but it took a long time, and then it took a long time to record it. Basically, the backing tracks were recorded in Italy in a castle, then we went to London, and then we came back here to LA. There was Trevor Horn, and then there wasn't Trevor Horn, and then Trevor Rabin was producing the album. You know, it took a long time!

JK: After all this time, I suppose you wanted to get the album done and finished and get out and play live again.

TK: Yeah, but I was enjoying life at that time too. It was sort of a time to kick back and just not be on the road, but the challenge was to write an album that would follow up a pretty big album, and that was not easy.

JK: No, I don't think any artist would find it easy following up an album of the magnitude of *90125*, but I think Yes did a very good job. It's not everyone's favourite Yes album, but I think there is some pretty good stuff on that album.

TK: Yeah, it was different, and the sum of its parts with it being in England. There was a sort of English music revolution going on with bands like ABC and Frankie Goes To Hollywood. That whole thing was happening in London, and there was Grace Jones and drum machines.

JK: And of course, Trevor Horn was right in the middle of that producing all those bands and artists, wasn't he?

TK: Oh, yeah. It was all around us as an influence, so that progressive rock thing that was Yes of the 70s was being influenced by that and the pop sensibility writing of Trevor Rabin. But it did have a lot of Yes to it as well; it was just way more commercial.

JK: After the tour to promote *Big Generator*, Jon left the band again, and there was another long period between albums. Jon went off and did Anderson Bruford Wakeman Howe, and then the next thing we hear about Yes is the *Union* thing. I have spoken to all the other guys involved in that, and even Bill Bruford enjoyed it.

TK: Really? Well, that is strange coming from Bill.

JK: Well, I am talking about the tour, and he said the tour was very enjoyable.

TK: Well, a lot of the pressure was off with there being so many people in the band. You do your thing, but you're not totally carrying everything, and I think everyone sort of felt that. Obviously Chris and Jon were on their own, but there were two drummers, two guitarists, and two keyboard players. It was a case of playing a lot of stuff from the 70s heyday too, which was a lot easier with all those people in the band. Actually, I really understand where Bill is coming from; it was a really fun time.

JK: I also spoke to Rick Wakeman, and he said, "It was weird because, with some of the older stuff I had to play when I first went into Yes when we did the *Union* tour, I found out from Tony that I had been playing it wrong for years."

TK: (*Laughs*) I know! Actually, it was only one piece of music from my day, from *The Yes Album* – "Yours Is No Disgrace." (*Laughs*) He came up to me one day and said, "I've been playing it wrong for all these years! I never knew it went like that!"

JK: I think it is nice to hear something like that when you compare notes like that. I also think in a situation like that you will always find a piece of common ground.

TK: Well, yes; and we had to. But I hadn't previously met Rick. All those years he had been in the band, and because I had lived here and I didn't go back that often, I wasn't part of that scene, so the *Union* tour was the first time I met him. And he is really just such a cool guy, very funny, of course, as you Brits know. I have only seen clips of his TV shows, and he is a funny guy! But, you know, it was great that everyone got on well and had fun.

JK: After the *Union* album and tour, there was a return to the *90125* line-up for the *Talk* album in 1994, which was your final album.

TK: Yeah, right.

JK: What are your thoughts on that, now that it is almost 20 years old?

TK: I know! Can you believe it? Well, *Talk* was fun to make. Basically, it's Trevor's album. Jon and Trevor decided to get together to write the nucleus of the album. So they wrote a bunch of things, which were all done at Trevor's studio, and really no one else was here. Alan wasn't here, Chris wasn't here, and Trevor and I were the only ones in the studio for a long time. We did the drum tracks and the backing tracks at a studio in Hollywood and then took them back to Trevor's studio. The interesting thing about that album was that it was the beginning of digital recording, and Trevor got one of the first digital performer studios together. It was a very interesting time breaking into that whole new technology.

JK: I suppose, as an artist, you are only usually thinking about what you are working on now. It is only when people like me come along and ask, "What was it like in 1971 when you played Crystal Palace" and things like that that make you think about the past. Talking to you, you seem very proud of what you have done. You are pretty cool with your past, whereas some artists aren't always cool with that because things might have been different under certain circumstances. But you seem pretty relaxed and at ease with your past.

TK: Yeah, well, I don't really take it so seriously. I think music should be enjoyed when making it. It can be hard, and in a band, it can be difficult with some egos and personalities. But I just feel lucky that so much of my past with Yes – although it was sporadic in a lot of ways – was important and enjoyable, and I look back on it with no regrets. I had fun with everyone. Everyone in the band is a character, and it was a great time. I don't look at that so seriously.

JK: You made some great music with Yes and other bands over the years, but with Circa you are still making great music.

TK: Well, yes. You know, the years have gone by, and I'm well past 65, but I feel that every day is an important day to make music. And fortunately, I have a musical partner who is way younger than I am. We've been friends from before the *Talk* tour when Billy first came on tour with Yes, but I have known him since 1987. We are just like two peas in a pod, and he is such an amazing musician and a hard worker. It is really easy to make music with him.

JK: So it's all good then?

TK: Yeah, it's all good. It's still fun to make music and play live, and we have a really, really cool band now. Scott Connor is just an amazing drummer and a great guy. There are no stupid egos in this band; we're just tied at the hip, which is really great. We have a new bass player, and he's really good and a cool guy. I think it really could be a very good time for Circa in a year or two.

JK: Well, the fact that you are still enjoying it is the main thing, I guess.

TK: Yeah, it is important. It gets tough out there on the road, and at my age, it is a little more difficult.

Tony Kaye left Yes following the tour to support the *Talk* album. Since then, he has been involved in a number of Yes-related projects with other former and current members of Yes. Initially, he was a member of Yes alongside other Yes men Billy Sherwood and Alan White. Alan White left to concentrate on his Yes obligations, and Billy and Tony continued with Circa. So far, the band have recorded three studio albums and a live DVD. Tony was also a member of the short-lived Yoso, which featured former Toto vocalist Bobby Kimball alongside Tony and Billy Sherwood. Circa, however, re-convened once the Yoso album and tour were completed, and in the summer of 2012, Circa played concerts in South America.

In 2018, Tony Kaye returned to Yes and played alongside Geoff Downes to celebrate the band's 50th Anniversary. He also played with the band in

early 2019, during the annual Cruise To The Edge.

Billy Sherwood: Beyond Yes
April 2012

Billy Sherwood probably first came to major prominence when he was put in the frame to replace Jon Anderson in Yes in 1990. Of course, the truth is that Billy never sought the position, although he did like working with Chris Squire, bassist and founding member of Yes. Billy worked with Yes on a number of albums, including the *Keys To Ascension II* album before finally being invited to join the band in 1997 for the *Open Your Eyes* album. Billy stayed with the band from 1997 until 2000 and recorded the studio album *The Ladder* and the live album *House Of Yes: Live From House Of Blues*. He then continued with his solo albums and Circa, the band that also initially included Alan White and Tony Kaye. The core of the band nowadays is Sherwood and Kaye.

Following Chris Squire's announcement that he was ill in 2015, Billy returned to Yes at Squire's request. Following Chris' death, Billy joined Yes permanently, where he remains to this day.

Jon Kirkman (JK): Hi Billy. Thanks for agreeing to do the interview. I really appreciate it!

The most recent album from you as a solo artist is *What Was The Question?*. You are, however, incredibly busy with a number of projects. So the first question must be, how easy is it moving from one project to another in what seems quick successions?

Billy Sherwood (BS): For me, it's very easy; I love working on music. I spend hours and hours in the studio, so I manage to get a lot done. I own my own place, so if I get the urge at 3AM to create, I can.

JK: *What Was The Question?* is a solo album in the true sense of the word, in that you wrote it, produced it, and played all the instruments on the album. How long does a project like this take from start to finish?

BS: It depends – anywhere from six months to a year. I collect ideas as I work on stuff. Mid-way through overdubbing a guitar part on something, I may get an idea for a riff or chord progression. I record it, grab the idea, and put it into a folder called "new ideas." That folder becomes the genesis of the solo records.

JK: You must be pretty confident in what you are doing to make a solo album this way. It has been said by some artists that work this way that it is a selfish way of working. You become really focused on what you do and therefore don't need the input of anyone else. Would this be true for you, or do you ask other people's opinions when working on an album like *What Was The Question?*

BS: I don't have people to bounce off; I am alone in my studio. I do what pleases me, and so by doing so, it pleases others. It is a selfish act to create a solo record the way I do, but at the same time, releasing it takes all that away. It then becomes something to share. It has become a tradition now for me to make these records alone. I enjoy it because I do work with a lot of other artists on various projects. I never really get a chance to be completely alone in any other area of music.

JK: John Wetton guests on the song "Delta Sierra Juliet." Was that the original idea, or were you going to originally sing that yourself?

BS: I planned to do it myself until I had Wetton in my studio. I was producing his solo CD *Raised In Captivity* at the time, and I thought, *How cool would it be to have John sing the title of the song*? I asked, he did it, and so you have it.

JK: Take us through the recording process then, of say a song like the title track. How would you go about laying that down? What do you start with first, and how do you build it up?

BS: For the title track, I had the guitar melody play through the entire song; it starts the song and carries on throughout. With that, I wanted to write it so that the riff would go through a series of alternate changes around it as it evolved. With that, I worked out the chords. I had the drum groove in mind as well, so I went with it. Songs always come from different inspirations; that track started with the guitar riff.

JK: The feel I get from this album is actually that it is not a solo album, but rather, it sounds like a group. How hard is it to convey a feeling like that over to the listener?

BS: I always record to make things feel as if there is a band in a room playing together. To that end, my solo stuff feels like a group of people, rather than sterilized overdubs. I like the natural feel of drums, basses, and guitars all working off each other. Since I play it all, I have a vision in my head with regards to the relationship between the drums and bass, vocals, and instrumentation. And all of that goes into making it what it is.

JK: I have noticed that vocals are very important on your recordings. The harmonies are very layered, which gives an amazing sound to the album. Do you have an inspiration vocally that you have modelled this style on over the years? Obviously, around the time of the Yes album *Open Your Eyes* I became very aware of this style, which integrated into the Yes sound very well.

BS: Yes is, of course, a big inspiration. That being said, there are many other places I turn to for vocal inspirations. Take 6 and Singers Unlimited come to mind – talk about vocal arrangements! Those groups raise the bar for singing. For me, I love vocals, and can't help myself but to sing, and then add more and more until it is, as you mentioned, layered. I love to sing. This genre of music I live in affords me the chance to really go for it with vocals.

JK: You have a couple of other projects in the works at the moment. There is a Supertramp tribute album, which has some interesting friends playing on it. So, first of all, how do you pick which songs you will include on the album, and how do you decide who will sing or play on each track?

BS: The label decides the projects and songs; I just do the work. That said, I love the work. I get to revisit some of the coolest records ever made and design an all-star cast. It's a very cool thing to be able to do.

JK: At one point, Roger Hodgson was considered as a replacement for Jon Anderson in Yes. Did you have any input on that suggestion? I know Roger wrote a song that appeared on *Talk*.

BS: No, I don't know anything about that. I know he is a friend of Trevor Rabin's.

JK: The other project you are currently working on is *The Prog Collective*, an album of songs written by yourself and performed by some of the biggest names in progressive rock music, including Rick Wakeman, Chris Squire, Annie Haslam, and Geoff Downes, just to name a few. I realise that in this day and age, files can be sent via email, and this makes the making of an album like this a little simpler than it would have been, say, 30 years ago. But even so, this seems like a mammoth task. Was there a time while in the middle of this project where you thought, *Maybe I have taken on too much*? (*Laughs*)

BS: The record came out great. I'm delivering it to the label today, as a matter of fact. I think any fans of the stuff I do will instantly get into it. It's loaded with cool artists, and the material is very interesting, musical, and dynamic. I am very proud of how it turned out. I never feel I've taken on too much. I love what I do and love the challenge of producing something on that scale.

JK: Of course, it is great to be able to do projects like this, but are you interested in live work? I know Circa, another one of your projects with former Yes keyboardist Tony Kaye, played a very important concert at the start of the year over the internet. Does that kind of one-off concert appeal more to you, or would you be interested in taking Circa out on the road for an extended tour?

BS: We wanted to do that u-stream show to get the band out there – get seen by those who keep asking, "When are you coming here or there?" That said, live is live, and of course, having an audience in front of you is always great. We are going to do some shows back east this summer in June. I always want Circa to move forward, live in-studio, etc. Out of everything going on, Circa is my baby, as it is Tony Kaye's. www.circahq.com is where anyone interested can find the CDs and DVDs.

JK: With Circa, you have worked on three albums, and the band has evolved into the current line-up, which includes yourself, Tony Kaye, and multi-instrumentalist Johnny Bruhns. Do you think Circa is progressing the way you originally saw it, and what is next for the band?

BS: Bands evolve in unique ways; often, when you least expect it. To that end, we have switched up the line-up. I decide to play lead guitar and hand over the bass role to Ricky Rat, an amazing player here in LA, who I've played with in developing my solo band – something that is going on behind the scenes. I was so impressed with his playing that for the first time, I started picturing playing the guitar for Circa. Although we have had various members, I tended to play a lot of the guitars on the studio recordings. With that in mind, we have yet again moved the evolution of Circa forward.

JK: You have performed Yes songs with Circa. Do you see a time when you will solely perform Circa songs, or will the Yes connection always come into play?

BS: Funny you should mention that...the new Circa set we are putting together will not include any Yes. We had always come up against a promotor asking us to play it, but as of this new formation and new gig wave coming, we decided to put out foot down and simply say "No!" (*Laughs*) I love Yes music, but at this point, Circa has plenty to play, and I would rather play the band's music live, and so it shall be done.

JK: Do you think you will ever tour as a solo artist, say, under the Billy Sherwood Band name, or do you prefer group projects like Circa or Yoso?

BS: I'm building a band as we speak, so you never know.

JK: You seem very prolific with so many different projects, either during creating or about to be released. So the question I have to ask is, how easy is it keeping all the balls in the air, for want of a better saying, as juggling would seem to be a major part of what you do musically?

BS: It comes naturally. I am always into making music. I don't think of it as anything other than doing my thing.

JK: What is next for Billy Sherwood, either as a member of Circa, a solo artist, or producer?

BS: More production, more Circa, more solo music, more live gigs with Circa, and always looking for what's next. Anyone looking for what's going on can follow me on Twitter or Facebook. I admin both and answer all my emails personally. As a result, a lot of artists working on their music have made contact for me to do work on their projects, either as a musician or an engineer. I love working on music, so don't be shy. If you need anything, I am here. The studio is open for business, not just for rock stars! (*Laughs*) Anyone interested in the solo music can find it at www.billysherwood.com.

JK: Thanks for taking the time to talk to me today, Billy. I really appreciate it.

BS: My pleasure. Cheers, Jon!

Following this interview, Billy would go on to record and produce an album with Star Trek actor William Shatner. In addition to his work with Yes, Billy also stood in for Asia bassist John Wetton for an American tour when John was sidelined by a serious illness. Unfortunately, John subsequently died from the illness on January 31st, 2017. Billy continues to record and play with Yes and Asia, and also records his own solo albums. He also still remains with Circa, alongside Tony Kaye.

Chris Squire: Fish Out Of Water
November 2006

In November 2006, I was contacted to see if I would be interested in conducting a filmed interview with Chris Squire about his solo album *Fish Out Of Water*. Replying in the affirmative, I travelled to Chris' house in London, and we settled down to have a chat. I had a rare 7" single, which contained an edit and remix of the track "Lucky Seven." The remix was done by Atlantic House producer Tom Dowd, who was famous for his work with Cream, Eric Clapton, Wishbone Ash, Lynyrd Skynyrd, and Rod Stewart. Chris was amazed that I had the single, as he was not aware of it. He said that record companies quite often did things like that to promote albums and that it was a nice surprise to find it. Since mine was a pristine copy, Chris asked if he could borrow it, and it eventually ended up on the re-mastered edition of *Fish Out Of Water* when it was reissued in early 2007. We then settled down to have a long chat about *Fish Out Of Water*.

Jon Kirkman (JK): Thirty-one years on from the original release of *Fish Out Of Water*, we are looking at a sort of revamped version of it. In fact, it is 31 years this month as we are talking – November 2006.

Chris Squire (CS): Yes! Thirty-one years! Strangely enough, it is the only solo album I have ever made, although I have started work on another one – we will talk about that later. So, it has been out there for 31 years. It came out in 1975, and it did extremely well at the time; it did about half a million albums worldwide.

JK: It went into the charts in America and in the UK, which was pretty good.

CS: Yeah, it was. Those were very pioneering sort of days because none of us knew exactly what we were doing, and it hadn't been long since 24-track recording had been available. I had just moved into my house in Surrey, where I had put together a studio in the basement. It was all part of the same project, really. I had bought some equipment from the MCI Company in Florida, like a mixing desk and a tape-recording machine. I bought a half-inch and a quarter-inch tape machine as well and put together my own studio. I did a lot of the wiring and stuff myself, along with obviously the people who knew how it should be wired! (*Laughs*) So the whole project was about finishing the studio in the house and then making this album.

JK: If we backtrack a little before then, the initial idea to do the album was quite interesting. At that time, Yes were one of the biggest rock bands in the world, and suddenly they are all going to take nine months off, and all make solo albums. Everyone said that the band was not going to split but that this was going to be an addition, and then they would come back as Yes. That was quite pioneering then because not many bands had done that, really. So where did the idea come from?

CS: Well, I can say that it wasn't the most popular idea up at Atlantic Records – that's for sure! I guess they smelled the idea of disintegration. This was reflected a little bit in their promotion efforts. They didn't go to great lengths to promote the albums they had with Atlantic. Of course, Rick Wakeman was on A&M, and they did do a lot of promotion for him. Not many people know this, but I think Rick sold about 30 million albums between *The Six Wives Of Henry VIII* and *Journey To The Centre Of The Earth*, so he was well in the lead in those stakes in terms of sales. The rest of us were with Atlantic, and I guess they probably didn't want to have too much solo success going on. They had had experience with Crosby, Stills, and Nash, and they could smell when people were getting itchy and wanted to break up the corporate thing, you know.

JK: I suppose what record companies see is five times more product for five times less the money coming in, so in some ways that is understandable. At the same time, it is great for the artist because you have still got Yes to come back to and your own thing, which sees a release for your own artistry.

CS: For us, it was a safety valve, and we were all very interested in recording. I know Jon had recording facilities in his garage at his house, and to a lesser extent, Steve Howe used the commercial studios more. It was that era when everyone was getting into wanting their own recording facility at home.

JK: I can remember reading some of the reviews. In fact, it was probably the Melody Maker, which was "the" paper to read if you wanted to take serious music into account, and thinking that this was the most Yes-like album. Well, he is actually in Yes, so…a little bit like Yes! So, it was stating the obvious somewhat. To be fair, your bass sound is very, very distinctive. Can we talk a little bit about your style and how you came to develop it?

CS: The strange thing is that the style I suppose I became best known for was because it was on our most successful single at that time – the bass riff on "Roundabout." It was really loud in the mix by Eddie Offord, and also what a lot of people did not realise at the time was that I also played the bass part on a guitar an octave higher and mixed that in as well. So, people thought it was my original bass sound. It wasn't exactly just a Rickenbacker bass sound; it was two guitars.

JK: But the Rickenbacker sound is very distinctive as well. For example, I know that John Entwistle played a Rickenbacker in the early days, as did Peter Quaife of the Kinks. Paul McCartney did as well, although he just sounds like Paul McCartney whatever he plays!

CS: To some extent, that applies to anyone. Over the years I have had quite a collection of guitars, and people have always said to me, whether I have been playing a Fender Jazz or a Gibson, it all sounds like me anyway. Interestingly enough, on the *Fish Out Of Water* album, I was actually experimenting with different sounds from the ones that I had become known for, like the twangy, trebly "Roundabout" sound. On "Hold Out Your Hand" and "You By My Side," the first two tracks, I actually went for more of a Jack Bruce kind of sound – not with so much high treble, but more a middy kind of sound that Jack Bruce was known for. Of course, he was one of my great influences, as was McCartney, who you mentioned, and Entwistle, who was probably the most influential. To an extent, Bill Wyman was an influence on me as well. It was a great time to be a young bass player because of all these great people who had great schemes and styles of their own that you could borrow from.

JK: There are a lot of good books about Yes on the market, and some are very scholarly and are like reading a textbook or manual on something. I remember reading one that compared your bass playing to John Coltrane and Hendrix, and I thought, *God, he has got to be pleased with that!*

CS: I know the guy you are talking about, and when I read it, I thought *Wow, okay.*

JK: Having got that accolade under your belt, I suppose the sky is the limit, really.

CS: In fact, that comment wasn't made about me until the 1980s when that book came out – or maybe even in the 90s. The 70s were just a very exciting time. I was in my 20s, and everything was just, "The sky's the limit! Let's just try to do what we can." Of course, we were getting great critical acclaim from papers like the Melody Maker and the NME. It became a bit of a joke after a while with the poll winning.

JK: Yeah, you wouldn't put bets on it because they wouldn't take bets on who was going to win, would they?

CS: No! There was one Melody Maker award that was being given out by Peter Cook and Dudley Moore, and it was the year they decided to have these ceramic balls that had Melody Maker inside them. They were on a little pole, which was on a little stand. When Peter Cook and Dudley Moore realised that between the two of us (Steve Howe and myself), were the Yes arrangers, bass player, guitar player, etc., and we had about nine of these, they said, "We'll just get this out of the way all at once." The balls were unfortunately not attached to the cylinders, so, of course, we dropped them all! I remember spending the rest of that day with Peter Cook. It was one of those days that was very entertaining. He was one of my favourite comedians of all time, so being in the back of a Daimler limo with him was quite a thrill for me.

JK: If we look at the album *Fish Out Of Water* then, once the decision had been made to record it, how quickly did the songwriting come together? I have always wondered if there are any tracks on that album that might have been considered for a Yes album, had Yes made an album at that point.

CS: In actual fact, one of the tracks did show up on *Going For the One*. One of the contenders for *Fish Out Of Water* was "Parallels". We recorded *Going For The One* in 1976-1977 over the winter, which was only a year afterwards. So that track had been a contender, but there wasn't enough time. The album was pretty full; it was about 20 minutes a side.

JK: It is 42 minutes, which for vinyl at the time was pushing the limit.

CS: I had a great engineer, Greg Jackman, who was the brother of Andrew Jackman, who made the orchestral arrangements.

JK: He had been in the Syn with you as well.

CS: I had known Andrew since I was five years old. We were born on the same block in Kingsbury, which is next to Wembley. We spent all of our young days together in the church choir, and I knew all of the brothers. Andrew was a bit older than me. As I said, Greg became the engineer and Jeremy, the middle brother, was the guy who founded the Kings Singers. So, they were a very musical family; their dad, Bill Jackman, was in the LSO as a clarinet player.

JK: One of the things that I noticed about *Fish Out Of Water* was the incredible orchestrations. Andrew's arrangements are just stunning.

CS: They are stunning, and I am so lucky that we cornered that market in time, at a time when my composing was developing. Andrew was an incredible character. He strove to lay claim for himself as a modern-day classical composer, but he didn't mind going in to do sessions for the Sex Pistols as well – and he did! He actually did arrangements on "Who Killed Bambi." He was an incredible person to work with, and looking back, a lot of the original elements of the orchestration came from his head as well. I told him he should get a credit for co-writing them, but he insisted it was fine and that he would just take the arrangement fee.

JK: As a friend of yours, he obviously didn't take advantage. There are people who would have taken advantage of a situation like that.

CS: Well, we had known one another for so long that it was natural for us to sit around, him on the piano and me playing bass, and work things out. I used to do sessions for him because he used to do those six songs in three hours for Ronco, you know. He would make the arrangements for those and put me in for £50 or something, or whatever it was in the 60s.

JK: I am sure that would be an interesting thing for the Yes collectors to track down. Do you remember any of the songs you did?

CS: Oh, there would never be any credit, but I do remember them. There were things like cover versions of Amen Corner and stuff like that.

JK: So you heard it here, then! Chris Squire is on a Top of the Pops album!

CS: Yeah, well, for Woolworths, for sure. We were in the Syn at that time, and he liked to write the more complicated bass part because that was getting him recognised as a good pop arranger. But there was never the time for anyone to learn it properly. I used to go around to his house the day before and learn the bass part. That would make me look more competent as all these other guys would be reading it as they were playing the sessions!

JK: You also have a former member of the band in, Bill Bruford, and a current member, Patrick Moraz, on the album. Was that deliberate?

CS: It was always weird to me when Bill left at the end of recording *Close To The Edge* because I kept looking at him thinking, *Let me go through this, you are an economics major, yet you don't quite understand that you are making more money now and you want to leave!* He was just bitten by this jazz bug, and he wanted to go away and play more jazzier electric stuff with Bob Fripp. That was what he wanted to do because Bill was a dyed-in-the-wool jazz guy. So, he left Yes, Alan White came in, and it all worked out. When I came to do *Fish Out Of Water*, I thought that it made sense because I had had all of these years playing with Bill. So, I asked him if he wanted to come and play on it and he was happy to.

JK: Do you think that is why many of the critics and others who reviewed the album said that it was the most Yes-like album of the solo albums?

CS: Probably. This was the Yes rhythm section up until *Close To The Edge*. He was a very unique drummer, which made it possible for me to be a more unique bass player, I suppose, in the way that our styles developed. He didn't play like other drummers a lot of the time. He played in a jazz way, and he used his bass drum to play accents with his snare drum as his bass drum. That gave opportunity to various Yes producers, and Eddie Offord when he came in as an engineer, to make the bass more like the drums. He was decorating what I was doing. It was a match that probably happened by accident, and resulted in the way I played and the way it was mixed.

JK: You put a guitar on the album, and I have noticed that a lot of bass players are sometimes frustrated guitar players. Is that the case for you?

CS: Well, no. I have never had any illusions about myself as a guitar player, but I did know that I could play as well as Neil Young! (*Laughs*)

JK: With respect to Neil Young, of course!

CS: At the time I was just fascinated by his style and everything he was doing; you know, that funky way of playing electric guitar. So, there is a bit of that on the end of "Silently Falling," and there is just a bit of scale picking or chord picking on the "Safe" song. What stands out about that album is that that is the only guitar on it. There was just a twelve-string Rickenbacker on those two tracks. There is no guitar anywhere else on the album, which of course, is unusual for a rock and roll album.

JK: Let's look at some of the tracks. The opening two tracks run into each other – "Hold Out Your Hand" and "You By My Side." Was that the way you wrote them, or did that come when you were scheduling the album and putting the tracks down to see what goes where? Was it maybe a later decision in the mix, or was it definitely decided that those two songs went together?

CS: I am pretty sure at a certain point when we were working on those two songs that we agreed to link them. We had to have a lot of stuff organised because Andrew then went on to orchestrate it for the orchestra, and we pretty much had the whole of the London Symphony Orchestra on those sessions. Thanks to Andrew's Dad – who fixed the sessions and got them at a reasonable rate, even for those days when things were much cheaper than they are now – he got an even better deal than that. Andrew had worked in sessions with large groups like that. He knew how much time we had, and we budgeted it with the amount of time it would take to the amount he wrote. He pushed it a lot. He had worked with a lot of those guys before, and they were putting in extra effort because he was Bill's son. There was a good feeling around those whole sessions. When I was at the one three-hour session, all the major pieces were done in that session. I was amazed at being there and hearing it all happen in three hours, being transformed from bass, drums, and a guy on vocal, to that!

JK: The arrangements are incredibly impressive by any standards, and you must have thought, *Hey, we really have something here* when you were listening to that.

CS: Oh, yeah! Up until then, Andrew had just shown me dots on the manuscript. Although I could read a bit as a chorister, it wasn't until I heard them play it that I thought how amazing it was.

JK: It takes a certain talent to be able to look at something and then play it straight off anyway; it is a proper discipline, isn't it?

CS: To be able to go that one step further and write it down on a manuscript and know what it sounds like – well… I have met other people since who can do that, Trevor Rabin for example, but Andrew was the guy I grew up with, and I thought it was amazing that he could actually do this.

JK: Let's look at one of the other tracks on the album – the final track "Safe," which is the extended track. There is a whole lot of other stuff going on in there. Just when you think it is coming to an end, something else comes in. It is almost like a piece of modern classical music; there are movements in there. I really like that track, and I know that it is a favourite among a lot of the fans.

CS: Basically, the premise of that was it had so much length to go, and we were wondering if we should add another chorus here or verse here, and Andrew and I agreed that we should finish the song and make it a bit instrumental for the outro. I suggested that we make it like the fugues. I always liked the fugues, and that is the premise of how most of the end is based – in the fugues form.

JK: There is a piece at the very end – I was listening to it today, actually – and it reminds me a little bit of "A Day In The Life" with the chord, and then the coda with the bass comes in. And I thought, *Wow! That is really interesting.* Just when you think it is finishing, there is just that little bit more to surprise you.

CS: Well, that was something that was just an afterthought, and I think it was because I always felt guilty about adding anything on the end of the big finish. I remember I was interested in how that came about. I was fiddling around in the studio with a Gibson double neck that I had and still have. It was a bass, a brown wood one, and a six-string guitar, and I was messing around with having the guitar pickups on with the bass, and that is how that came about. That is actually what that is.

JK: It was a nice surprise at the end of that. There is this chord that is just straining away, and then this picking comes out, and it is actually really nice.

CS: A lot of happy accidents happened on that album.

JK: Sometimes, the best moments are just accidents, aren't they? If you had contrived to do that, it wouldn't have worked.

CS: Exactly. I have had a lot of them, especially during the Yes recordings, and you think, *Wow! Did we mean to do that? Let's keep it, though!*

JK: Just a couple of things. We have the album here that you signed for me on CD, and the photograph was taken by Brian Lane, the Yes manager. How did he manage to work his way into that?

CS: Believe it or not, it has been pulled down now, but that was the Detroit Hilton in Detroit in the States. The elevators were in the middle, and on either side was this metal latticework thing, either side of the two elevator doors. Brian Lane had just got one of those Polaroid cameras. He had gone and bought one that morning, and it was when they very first came out. He thought that for a laugh, he would stand at the elevator and take a picture of everyone as they got up in the morning. Fortunately, I do not look as if I just got up!

JK: It is a very unusual photograph though, and on a twelve-inch album it is very impressive!

CS: Well, it is just another one of those lucky things. Even the symmetry of the way my face is lined up with the metalwork is pure luck! I just got out of the elevator, stood like that, and he took the picture. It was done in one shot.

JK: Where is the stained glass from?

CS: That was a piece of stained glass that I bought from Lillian Nassau, an antique glass dealer in New York. It was made by Tiffany himself; it was a 3D glass thing. He was famous for making lampshades, really, but he made a few windows like that. The actual depth of field of the stained glass where the fish are hanging in the middle is actually thicker than the glass is surrounding them. I just bought it, really, and it ended up in my shower.

JK: Didn't that image come as a poster with initial copies of the album as well?

CS: Yeah, it did.

JK: I have a surprise for you! It is the promotional single for the track "Lucky Seven." First of all, it is totally different from anything else on the album. It sounds very American, and this particular version is an edit, which was made by no less a person than Tom Dowd, who is sadly no longer with us, but he was a very famous producer.

CS: I've never heard this!

JK: Stereo one side and mono the other side, so presumably mono for the AM stations and stereo for the FM stations.

CS: Yeah. This was obviously done as a promotional tool that Atlantic records put out there, and I guess put out to promote the album on the radio. I didn't know it existed, actually.

JK: What I find strange is that they picked the track that is so unlike the rest of the album to promote the album. It is not that it is bad, just that it is so unlike everything else on the album. I can imagine people hearing it, buying the album, and being puzzled as to why it is so different.

CS: Well, it is, really. I don't know why it went in that direction. It was just because it was kind of simple, and once again Bill Bruford's jazz influence came into it, and then I think because I felt it was heading in a slightly jazzy direction – it is in 7/4 time, hence the title "Lucky Seven" – I had Mel Collins come in and play on it. The sax is brilliant on it! I listened to it the other day, and the sax still stands up. Amazing, really. Is Mel still with us?

JK: Yeah, he is in the 21st Century Schizoid band, which is made up of ex-members of King Crimson. But the sax playing on that is wonderful!

CS: It is, isn't it? I remember it was pretty much a take one or maybe take two. He certainly just had a run through and then just did it.

JK: From what we have been discussing then, the album came together very quickly.

CS: It did, and once again, I think why it did was that Andrew was very organised. He made sure we dotted the I's and crossed the T's before we started getting people in. We got it done in a very business-like way, which also kept the enthusiasm bubbling pretty high because of the fact that it was moving along very quickly and everyone involved in it wasn't hanging around, which was good. Mel also plays baritone sax on "Silently Falling." The middle bit over the keyboard solo is very jazzy, and once again we are back to Patrick Moraz, which was your original point about Patrick being on the album! (*Laughs*)

Patrick made two very important contributions to the album, actually. One is a fantastic organ solo that he plays on that track, which was probably a few takes. We probably did a bit of mixing with take number one and number five, and that kind of thing, but it ended up sounding very cohesive and really good. And once again, Bill is driving it in a very jazz-like way.

The other extremely interesting thing Patrick brought to this album was that, as far as I know, it was the very first time anyone played a synth bass. Bear in mind, we are back in the days now just prior to when the Bee Gees did their disco thing, and I don't know where Patrick heard it, maybe on a disco record or something. When we were doing "Silently Falling," I said it would be nice if I were doing some noodling or twiddling around on the bass, and he said, "Well, I could play this bass line on my synthesizer." It was one of those, "Oh, can you do that?" moments.

JK: Another happy accident, then?

CS: Yeah, another happy accident. It is one of the first examples of a mini Moog playing a bass line. Maybe you could find an earlier example, but it was one of the first for sure before all the dance records came along.

JK: When the album came out it went into the Billboard Top 100, and over here in the UK it went into the Top 30 albums chart. That must have been very pleasing for you, but shortly after it came out in early 1976, the band got back together. I think it was spring 1976 and it was called *The Solos Tour*, which I presume was to promote the solo albums with Yes material. The problem is, after about a week all the solo material disappeared out of the set.

CS: (*Laughs*) Yeah! Well, it should have been called "The Good Intentions Tour." Yes rehearsals are always slightly chaotic because they were usually associated with some new Roger Dean stage set made out of fibreglass with lights and stuff. It was all pioneering stuff back in those days, so all our rehearsals in those days consisted of people walking about wearing masks and sawing and sanding things down as well as trying to play music. I don't know why we didn't do them in different buildings, but I think it was the whole camaraderie thing between the band and the crew, which is what we did in those days. What we did was draw up a set and probably never actually played it in its entirety until the first show. We all learned a bit from each other's solo albums to play, and we got round to the first show, and we found it ended up at just about five hours long! (*Laughs*)

JK: We are getting into Grateful Dead territory there then, aren't we? Which, I am sure the Yes fans would have loved, but as an artist you kind of flag somewhere in the middle with a set like that.

CS: Well, I'd seen the Grateful Dead around that period at the Rainbow because our lighting guy, Michael Tait, was on loan to them between touring with us. So, I went to see them, and I remember standing next to him on the side of the stage while they were playing. Michael was responsible for a lot of the Yes dynamics in terms of lighting for things like "Heart Of The Sunrise" and stuff like that. He was standing there for about 20 minutes, and he said, "Yeah, it's blue now, and then in twenty minutes it will be green for twenty minutes, and then I'll probably go red after that." So, they weren't big on production! (*Laughs*) But getting back to the Yes show, it was generally a more high-energy thing. And while you could do that with The Dead in that laid back Quaalude world, you couldn't really do that with Yes because it was a lot more of an active show at around three hours a show, which was something we used to do. That was about the maximum we wanted to do because it would have got boring after that.

JK: Two of the songs you did manage to do on a couple of the dates, which were
Hold Out Your Hand" and "You By My Side." You said that Jon was playing along on bass on those songs and that Jon is a great "joiner inner," so that must have been an interesting thing for you.

CS: Well, it was. I remember him asking what key it was in, and I said "A Flat," and I remember lending him my Paul McCartney Hofner Violin bass because I said we could try it. He could plonk along on some low notes while I played the high stuff, as it might sound good. I never really know if it did because it was fairly shambolic with all of us trying to do it. Of course, Patrick Moraz had not played on those particular songs, but he mimed on the video, so he knew a little more about it. I remember learning something from *Olias Of Sunhillow* and playing bass pedals and triggering stuff. It was quite involved trying to do these songs, and I think after a while we thought we couldn't sustain a show that was going on for that long.

JK: I can tell you it was about ten dates into the tour when there was a definite cut off and no more solo stuff in the set. It is not as if it petered out; it was a case of "Right there!"

CS: (*Laughs*) I'd like to hear one of the bootlegs one day and hear what Jon's bass playing was like.

JK: That tour was very special for a number of reasons. You played the JFK stadium, which was in front of 120,000-130,000 people. That was a huge audience!

CS: Yeah.

JK: How difficult is it to relate to an audience like that? It was a big show with Peter Frampton and Gary Wright on the bill with you headlining. It's one thing playing in perhaps the Rainbow, but when you are playing in a stadium, and the audience is back in the bleachers at the back...

CS: Yeah, and luckily, Peter Frampton had been booked to do this show prior to his album becoming so big so that obviously helped swell the audience. But I remember working it out that I was earning $5,000 a minute during the show, which wasn't bad, but I don't think it ever happened again! (*Laughs*)

JK: That was a very big and exciting tour, and yet after the tour there was another change in the line-up of Yes. It seemed to be a real peak, and then off again in another direction. *Going For The One* included "Parallels," which was previously earmarked for *Fish Out Of Water*.

CS: Yeah, "Parallels" had been a contender for *Fish Out Of Water*, but in the scheme of things it didn't really fit, so it found its way onto *Going For the One*, We recorded that album in Montreux, which was another exciting round of recording events.

JK: If I think about that now and that song, it makes perfect sense that it comes from the *Fish Out Of Water* sessions. I can actually imagine that track on the album.

CS: Yeah, it could have been. It would have been nice to have heard it orchestrated as well, but for some reason, there was never any orchestration done for it. But maybe one day I could do something like that with it.

JK: Well, the album is coming out again in an "all singing all dancing" version with some bonus tracks, and this interview will be on it as well. But I hear you are working on a new solo project as well, so that will be only your second solo album in 35 years! To be fair, you have been distracted by your work with Yes.

CS: (*Laughs*) Yeah, I know some of my partners have put out 130 solo albums. I won't mention who, but that is a little bit of overkill, maybe.

JK: I discussed this a few years ago with you, and at the time you said Andrew Jackman had just died. He played a very big part in the creation of this album, so I suppose you are never going to make another album that sounds like this.

CS: Not exactly like it, but I can tell you that the guy I was working with on keyboards in the recent Syn revival, Gerard Johnson, is very much from the same school as Andrew. Strangely enough, he is also a Catholic choirmaster as well, and he has also worked with the band Saint Etienne. So, he is a kind of well-rounded guy, and he loves, as we do, Andrew's work. I have been working with him, and strangely enough, while we haven't pushed the orchestral direction or anything, the things that have come to light are leaning in that direction. But they are different, and of course, it is 35 years later. We have the technology now to do so much more, and even hear it before we put real strings on it.

JK: What kind of a time scale are we looking at, then? At the moment, Yes are on what we call a "sabbatical," and we don't know how long that will last.

CS: Well, I do know that we are talking to each other to get together and do some work. I would like it to happen next year, although I have a suspicion that it won't happen until 2008 because of other people's bands.

JK: Which would fit in nicely with the 40th Anniversary of Yes.

CS: Exactly! So, I would be remiss not to use this time prior to that to get the second one underway. Believe it or not, I already have more than 29 minutes' worth of ideas.

With that, the interview was over, and we adjourned for something to eat. While there has not been a second solo album like *Fish Out Of Water*, Chris did release a Christmas album entitled *Chris Squire's Swiss Choir*. The album included a guest performance from Steve Hackett, which led to another studio project that developed into the group Squackett and the album *A Life Within A Day*, which was released in May 2012. So, as it stands, *Fish Out Of Water* remains Chris Squire's only bona fide solo album.

This interview in filmed format was part of the deluxe edition of *Fish Out Of Water*, which was released as a CD/DVD package in the summer of 2007. In 2018, the album was expanded again, this time into a multi-disc boxed set with a remix and DVD, and again this interview was included. Chris had asked me in 2014 to do a further interview, which would have taken us through the remix and 5.1 sessions. Sadly, Chris died before we could do that.

≈

Patrick Moraz: The Story Of *i*
April 2012

Patrick Moraz joined Yes in early 1974 and immediately set about recording the *Relayer* album with the band. There were a few rehearsals before the band headed out on the road to promote the *Relayer* album. Throughout 1975, the various members of Yes prepared solo albums for release, and by August 1975, Yes had finished what would turn out to be the first leg of the *Relayer* tour with an appearance at the Reading Festival. Almost immediately afterwards, Patrick flew to Brazil to begin recording his debut solo album. The framework for it had been worked on during the Yes tour, with the initial idea coming from a stay in a hotel in Nashville. The album, of course, was a concept album and would be released early in 1976 as *The Story of i*

Jon Kirkman (JK): There has been a lot of confusion over the years regarding the title of your first album. Some people just call it *i*, and others call it *The Story of i* Perhaps you could resolve this now by telling us how you titled the album.

Patrick Moraz (PM): At the time, it was *i*, and I was the first artist to go to the record company with the logo for *i*. It was something I had a vision for when I was between Geneva and London. I looked up into the sky one night, I think it was Christmas 1975, and saw this, and I also realised that it was the tenth letter of the Etruscan alphabet. Anyway, I decided that I was going to call the album this, and I went to the record label and told them. They weren't convinced and even said, "You can't call the album after a letter. Who is going to be interested in that? You won't do anything." And then they said, "Well, why don't you call it *i*, a.k.a. *The Story of i*" Of course, now we have "*i*" everything like iPad and iPod, etc. Anyway, it was registered at the Library of Congress and the PRS and everything as *i*, and that is why I wanted to call it *i* because it is *i* (*Laughs*).

JK: Well, thinking about the album when it came out, all the other Yes solo albums came out through Atlantic Records. But you had a deal with Charisma, which of course dated back to your Refugee days. So in effect, that probably gave you an edge because you weren't in competition with the other guys in Yes, who were all on the same label, and therefore would be fighting for attention.

PM: Right. You are probably correct in that, but *i* was also voted the "Best Album of the Year" in Keyboard Magazine, which was nice. *i* was also voted

"Best New Talent," and it was their first poll too, which was nice. I really wasn't expecting that, and I didn't even know that Keyboard Magazine existed at the time. I did an interview I think, but was certainly not expecting the award, particularly not the "Best Album of the Year." That probably means more to me than a lot of other things, possibly because it was also my first solo album.

JK: There is a concept and a story in *i*, which I won't go into now, as I am sure that everyone who has the album knows it, and it is widely available to read on the internet. But where did you get the inspiration for the story? It is an interesting one, isn't it?

PM: Well, you know some of it in the Hunger Games. Funnily enough, I was the precursor of the Hunger Games! (*Laughs*) So my album must have been noticed, as it is a similar kind of story, but with my story I just invented it.

JK: You have some incredible musicians playing on the album including two drummers. On one side of the album you have the amazing Alphonse Mouzon, who was in Weather Report, and then you have Andy Newmark. So, what was behind the decision to have two drummers on distinct parts of the album, as Alphonse plays on one side and Andy on the other?

PM: Well, partly it was because of the availability of time. But as you know, *I* is one piece really in two movements. But I wanted it to have a distinct approach rhythmically, in terms of the drumming. Alphonse I had seen actually with Larry Coryell at the time, rather than Weather Report. I contacted him and found he was available at that time, so I flew him in for ten days. Then Andy Newmark was available, and I wanted him for a specific piece at the start of side two or the second movement. And then I got him to play something that I should have asked Alphonse to play, but Andy was fantastic! He played it incredibly well, and of course, having played with Sly and the Family Stone, he was very well versed in what I was into. In fact, these sessions were probably an early chapter in world music, apart of course, from what Santana had done in the 60s. But this album has a more symphonic approach, I think. It's a more progressive "world" approach than Santana, which was purely commercial music at the time, which is very good and very successful, but I didn't want my music to be seen as just samba music because I had done the backing tracks in Brazil. So I used the percussion to have a very symphonic interaction with the drums, making it more progressive. But I would definitely have called it "world music" at the time.

JK: The bassist on the album, Jeff Berlin, is a guy with Yes connections, having played with Bill Bruford and Anderson Bruford Wakeman Howe. But your album was the first time I had come across the name. So where did you meet Jeff?

PM: I actually met Jeff in New York. He had just finished his studies at Berklee. He was a top student there, and I met him through Ray Gomez. Ray is the guitarist on my first two albums, *I* and *Out In The Sun*, and he was very instrumental in the choosing of the musicians on those albums. He was also responsible for some of the arrangements on those albums, and of course, his solos are absolutely brilliant. As far as I am concerned, Ray Gomez is one of the top guitarists in the world, ever. He is sometimes underrated, but his playing is absolutely out of this world. And at the time of this album, he was only about 25 or 26.

JK: Again, your album was the first time I had heard of Ray Gomez, but I remember he went on in the late 70s and 80s to have a high-profile solo career.

PM: Yeah, he did. But you can check him out on YouTube, and you will see just how good he is. I spent a lot of time with him over the years, and I can tell you he is just incredible and played beautifully on the album.

JK: You had the story, and I presume much of the music, mapped out before recording. So how long did it take for you to put together the album recording-wise?

PM: It took four months from September and three weeks into December, and then in January some overdubs, either in England or in Switzerland. So four months of actual recording, and of course, that included the three days recording backing tracks in Brazil.

JK: One of my favourite pieces on the album is the song "Best Years Of Our Lives," and many people were surprised that it wasn't successful as a single, as it was very commercial.

PM: Yeah, I was surprised as well, but that was not my decision. When you do a solo album, you leave things in the hands of the record company. I think in America it was released by Atlantic, and in the UK by Charisma. But it wasn't a single because… Well, I don't know. As I say, these things are never the decisions of the artist, really.

JK: The album as a whole is a very dense piece of music, and in the CD version, you included the production notes. You can see that there is a lot in the album, and it does stand the test of time. And with the advent of compact discs, you can hear so much that perhaps you might have missed on the original album.

PM: Well, I still play a lot of the music from the album when I perform solo concerts, or even if I play with a band. It is a great challenge to try and recreate those sounds, or those arrangements live, but even if I just play them on my own at a solo piano concert, I always include a version of "*Best Years Of Our Lives*" and "*Soon*" as well! (*Laughs*) I always play excerpts from the stuff I did with Yes. I love to play those pieces, but "*Best Years Of Our Lives*" is always there.

JK: When the album came out in June 1976, you were right in the middle of an American tour with Yes. Were you a little disappointed that you weren't able to give the album the proper promotional push due to your Yes commitments? Although, there were a few gigs where you all featured some music from the solo albums, wasn't there?

PM: Yes, that is correct. I think we did four or five gigs with Yes with everyone having a solo spot in the show. But, it was quickly decided that it would be better for Yes to play just Yes material, rather than feature stuff from the solo albums. It was a joint decision within the band, but I would have been quite happy playing the solo stuff I played on *Fish Out Of Water* and played on *Beginnings* with Steve. But yeah, I suppose it made sense to concentrate on Yes.

JK: As an album, I think *I* is begging for a big production with an orchestra, full production, and guest vocalist. Have you ever considered doing that, or has there ever been an offer on the table for you to do it?

PM: (*Laughs*) Well, the possibility to do a big production is one thing, but having the means to do it is another. If you have the means, you do it, but something like that would cost a great deal, of course.

JK: We talked some time ago, and you said you would like to do the *Future Memories* shows as well.

PM: Yeah, but the *Future Memories* was an instant composition filmed live, remember? So that wasn't a big production because it was an instant composition and composed live as we filmed. *The Story Of i* would be a much bigger and different thing.

JK: Okay. Here is a possibly difficult question to answer: over 35 years on, you have written and recorded a lot of other music in that period. Where do you see *I* in your canon of work?

PM: Well, of course, it stands as my first album, of which I am incredibly proud still. It is called *I*, and it has the logo on the front, and it is as I wanted it. I can play it live on stage if I want, but I think that album, *Out In The Sun*, and my third album *Patrick Moraz,* still stand the test of time and sound good and are among my most important work. Let's put it this way: I don't regret anything about that album, or the others that followed. But then again, I don't regret one note I have ever played in my life as a musician.

JK: That is a fair answer, as I do realise that it is like asking you which is your favourite child.

PM: Exactly. I have many favourite pieces over the years. In fact, somebody told me I had over 380 pieces of music on iTunes, so there is a lot out there! But *I* was my first solo album, and as such, that makes it special.

Patrick Moraz left Yes in late 1976 and continued to record solo albums and record and tour with the Moody Blues. He also worked with Bill Bruford as Moraz Bruford, and first met Bill Bruford at the sessions for *Fish Out Of Water*. **More recently, two live Moraz Bruford albums have been released:** *Music For Piano And Drums Live In Maryland* **(2005), and** *In Tokyo* **(2009). In 2012, Patrick released his own live solo album,** *Live At Abbey Road*. **He continues to record albums and perform solo concerts, and in 2018, Patrick appeared with Yes and performed "Soon." It was the first time Patrick has played with Yes since 1976.**

∽

Trevor Horn: Living In The Yes Age
May 2016

Yes released the *Drama* album in August 1980, and for many Yes fans, the album was a huge shock. The biggest shock was that Jon Anderson was no longer in the band. Trevor Horn had replaced Jon, and Geoff Downes had replaced Rick Wakeman. Trevor and Geoff had been a pop duo called the Buggles, who had a lot of success in 1979, both as producers and with a worldwide hit, "Video Killed The Radio Star." Following the UK tour for *Drama*, however, the band split. The next time Yes resurfaced, they were with a new line-up and a new album, *90125*, which was produced by Trevor Horn.

Fast forward to 2016: Yes embarked on a tour that featured the *Drama* album in its entirety. Trevor Horn appeared with the band during two shows in the UK to sing "Tempus Fugit," one being Oxford, the other being the Royal Albert Hall. Following the tour, I met Trevor at his studio to discuss his time with Yes. There were a few surprises for me as the day unfolded, as you can hear in this interview.

Jon Kirkman (JK): 1979 was a big year for you. The Buggles were doing very well. You had a number-one hit single, "Video Killed The Radio Star." You were doing a lot of production work as well. I can remember Dan-I, The Jags, remixing stuff like that...

Trevor Horn (TH): Those were the two. We did those two, yes. And then what happened was, we decided we needed to get a manager, and my wife had known Brian Lane. So, we got Brian Lane as our manager, you know, partly because I'd seen Brian Lane's name on all of the Yes albums. Part of it was because I knew he'd managed Yes, and my brother and I were like, huge Yes fans all the way through the 70s. I was just a big fan of the band. I mean, how could you be a musician, a bass player, and not be? And I loved Jon Anderson's voice. I mean, the very first time I was actually aware of Yes, I was living in Margate. I went to the pub with my girlfriend, and there was a local band up, and they were sort of ripping various people off and then they did this song, (*Sings*) "I've seen all good people turn their heads each day..." I was like, "Fuck me, that's a good song! Did they write this?" And somebody said, "No, that's a song by a group called Yes. You'd like them." And I was like, "Well, I like that song. That's really good writing; that was brilliant." And of course, I bought *The Yes Album*, and I was totally hooked. I mean, the bass part, you know? I'd never heard a bass sound like that before. "Starship Trooper"...I wore the record out. So from then on, I was a fan. I bought their earlier albums, and I went to see them in 1975 on the *Yesterdays* tour in Leicester, and they were great! I remember standing at the end of "And You and I" because it reached such a climax, you know, and in a way, the only thing I'd seen like that was Pink Floyd. I saw Pink Floyd in 1968 doing the *Ummagumma* stuff in Blackpool, and they were like nobody else, you know? Yes were kind of like nobody else too. You couldn't really categorise them.

JK: No.

TH: So, in 1979, I had a hit. You've got to realise I was a bass player. I wasn't really a singer, you know? I was always the guy that sang one song at the end of the evening, you know, or something like that. When I was singing in bands, they always had me singing Brian Ferry, because he sang out of tune. So they said, "You sing out of tune. So…"

Yes, we get Brian Lane as our manager and, I think, *Well, I know what's going to happen. I'm going to meet Chris Squire, and I'm going to meet the band. That's quite exciting!* So, sure enough, I met Chris Squire in Brian's office and… because Chris… when you first meet him, he's pretty deceptive because he sort of talks slowly, you know. And he invited us down to his place in Virginia Water, Geoff and I. So, we went down to see him one evening. The funny thing was, we were kind of…in awe. Geoff and I played together a lot in crummy bands, top 40 bands, stuff like that as well. Going down to meet somebody from Yes, you know, who lived in a kind of mansion…his wife had hair down practically to the floor. It was quite an interesting experience. And what was quite funny at the time was that his kids were waiting outside to meet us because we were the sort of pop stars of the day.

JK: Of course! The Buggles had recently had a number-one single, which in the UK was a big deal.

TH: Yeah, and so we had to do sort of autographs and a meet-and-greet with the kids and then we hung with Chris. And then, you know, I was probably burbling on about what a Yes fan I was, and I said, "You know, I wrote this song for Yes," and he said, "Play it to me." So, I played him "Fly From Here," and he was like, "Hmm, you sound a bit like Jon Anderson." I said, "Yes." He said, "Why don't you come down, both of you, and run it with the band?" And I was like, "Yes, but Jon…you know, Jon might sing it, you know?" And he was like, "No, just come and work it out anyway." Geoff and I went down and started playing with the three of them. It was just the three of them there in a rehearsal room.

JK: Did you not think it odd that there was only the three? Did bells not start ringing at that point?

TH: No, not straight away, I have to be honest. And we worked on "Fly From Here" a bit, and I suppose pretty quickly we all got along, you know what I mean?

JK: Yes.

TH: Chris was a fan of The Buggles. He really liked the production on "Living In The Plastic Age," that particular track. He used to keep playing it, and he kind of wanted to do something like that, but obviously that… Yes. Then the idea, you know…after we'd done this song, then I found out that they'd had a…they'd been in "broyges" with Jon. That's a Yiddish word for an argument, and whatever. And Jon wasn't coming back, and neither was Rick and then it was suddenly, "Do you and Geoff want to join the band?" And I was like, "What? You've got this tour booked in America; 44 shows, you know? It's like, three nights at Madison Square Garden. I mean, this is…I'm going to be a worm on the end of a pin on that one!" But, you know, I suppose Steve and Alan were pretty encouraging. I always got on really well with Steve and Alan. I always really liked them. So, I remember going into a room and telling my wife, "I am not doing this," and then coming out of the room and saying, "I'm going to do it!" (*Laughs*)

JK: Chris once said to me, "I spent ages telling him, 'You can do it! You can do it!' Once I convinced him to do it, I then had to convince Jill that he could do it, which was a totally different thing. I have to say, I did spend a lot of time trying to convince him. In the end, he said, 'Okay, I'll give it a go,' then I had to convince Jill."

TH: Yes. So, of course by the time we finished *Drama*, you know, we all knew each other a lot better, and it seemed like it came out pretty well. We finished it, and it had a vibe to it. And pretty soon after we started recording it, Eddie Offord left. I'm sure you've heard some of the Eddie Offord stories…

JK: Well, I've heard lots of stories about Eddie Offord, and they're all amusing for different reasons, but how much of the album did he do? Wasn't he was brought in to do the backing tracks originally and then disappeared?

TH: I've got no idea because I kind of… You know, Geoff and I came on board and then it was a new experience for me, being the singer, because generally when you're the bass player, you're playing all the time because the track is the thing that goes down first. So, suddenly I was sitting around, so of course, what did I start doing? Producing. But we got a great sort of work with him going, you know? Like, the intro of "Machine Messiah" took us a day, you know, and the guys...it was all played, no short cuts in those days, just played...

JK: No Pro Tools then...

TH: No Pro Tools. And they would play it, and I was in the control room, and I'd give it marks out of ten and...but it was good. We were working together, you know what I mean? And we got somewhere that we were all happy with. "Machine Messiah" took us about four or five days working our way through it and then joining them together on the analogue.

JK: That's the Yes way.

TH: Yes.

JK: You must have heard the story about *Close to the Edge*.

TH: God, I can't even begin to think about it. I learned a lot, and I learned a lot from Chris and Steve because they did some things I'd never done before, like cutting around the two-inch.

JK: Yes. Well, they'd done that on *Close to the Edge*, and Bill Bruford remembers saying, "That's when I started to worry. When they were editing the two-inch, the multitrack tape, I'm thinking, *This is either going to be really good or just a complete car crash.*"

TH: It was really good, but Chris would do things. For instance, he'd say, "That bar's a bit loose. Let's just take a quarter of an inch out." I was like, "Fuck, yes, sure." It was kind of like early Pro Tools, but the band were playing so well it wasn't really difficult. Nothing was a problem, you know what I mean? Geoff was fucking brilliant back in 1979. If you listened to the Buggles, most of the Buggles's keyboards...it's all Geoff and the keyboards are, like, state of the art, really, for the day.

JK: Yes. They are.

TH: Even when Geoff was playing two or three wacky little keyboards, he was always better than anybody else because he always got them to sound great.

JK: Yes.

TH: And so we finished the album, and then, of course, we go and we start rehearsing, and I have to figure out which ones I can sing, which Yes songs that is, I can just about get through.

JK: Well, can I interrupt you there and just ask you about "Fly From Here," because, although that was your kind of in, there was no "Fly From Here" on the album. Geoff told me that you did do a demo of it and Bill Bruford played the drums on it.

TH: No. It was a guy called Paul Robinson.

JK: Was it? Okay.

TH: Bill Bruford played the drums on another track that I did with Bruce called "The Welder." I just hired him because I wanted to meet him, and he was nice. He was a good drummer. I was curious, but he's a jazz drummer. There's nothing wrong with that, but that was his thing. If you think about it, the sound of the early Yes albums before Alan joined was kind of different, you know, because of the way that Bill played the drums. But then, Alan brought a whole new thing to it. He had much more aggression in a certain kind of way, and a brilliant relationship between the hi-hat and the drums. And how he plays…that's really quite hard to quantify, unless you listen to drums a lot.

JK: Chris put it as they were poles apart. He said, "You've got Bill, who's coming from the jazz angle with the snap of a snare drum. And then, you've got the simplistic – not in a bad way – sort of drumming on "Imagine" from Alan. It's poles apart, but they both work within the Yes framework."

TH: Yes, but then you listen to that drum fill on "Instant Karma"…that fill shows you how much Alan really knows, you see. When we did that concert of mine in 2006, when I went to mix it, Alan's playing was brilliant. I was playing it to people saying, "Listen, that's the guy that played on "Imagine," yes? Listen to that, how right that sounds, you know?" But, you know, these days with drum machines it's so easy, to some degree, to recreate it. But when you hear it done by the real thing, wow!

JK: So, the album was recorded, it came out, and it did very well in the UK. It got to number two, which must have pleased you going into the band and the album does so well.

TH: Yes.

JK: Some of the reviews, however, were a little unkind. The British tour, definitely. I think one of the reviews – I think it was in Sounds [British music paper] actually – said, "Imagine Yes being fronted by Ronnie Corbett."

TH: Yes.

JK: And it's like, well, you expect that from the British press anyway because it's all about the jokes and about them.

TH: Well, you see, the real problem was, if I look back on it, I was totally inexperienced, and I went off on tour. We had two weeks of rehearsal, and we never played through the set once because Chris' gear kept breaking down. This is my first real taste of the sort of mad chaos that happens in a band, and so by the time, the first show came around, which was 15,000 people in Maple Leaf Gardens in Toronto. To say that I was frightened is an understatement. But I've always had this thought, you know, *Fuck it. It's only music, and I love music dearly.* But, you know, if you play it wrong, all it is, is a bit of wrong music, you know what I mean? It's not like you're a doctor doing an operation, you get it wrong, and somebody dies. So, whatever happens is going to happen. When I say we never got through a whole set, we really didn't. And at one point out of frustration, one of the crew, it was either Claude or Nunu, got on the mic and said, "You are fired from this band!" and all this kind of stuff at Chris. And Chris was just like, "Control your roadie, Steve." (*Laughs*) The first night when we went out on the stage at Maple Leaf Gardens, it was funny because as soon as I got on the stage, I didn't have anything planned in terms of what I was going to say. Of course, they only just told me before we went on, "You're going to do the talking." Fuck. I hadn't worked anything out! But once it got going, it was just like I'd been on stage all my life, so...

JK: What are your memories of the American tour?

TH: Well, my memories of it were that... Well, if I had known what I know now, 36 years later, I would have taken a singing teacher with me because I had no warm-up routine. I didn't...nobody taught me, and consequently, I was good; I was okay at the start. I heard a take somebody had done of the first show at Maple Leaf Gardens. It wasn't bad, you know. I'm clinging on, like, by my fingernails, you know, because the band is sort of compensating, obviously for the lack of Jon, by playing like hell. If you listen to any of the shows, they sound incredible musically...

JK: I've got lots of recordings.

TH: (*Laughs*) I imagine you have! Well, the band are amazing, really hard-core, and they were really nailing it all. And I'm just hanging on, and sometimes I hung on better than others. In retrospect, it would have been better if I had had a whole routine. There's stuff I should have done that I know about now that I didn't know about then. Bad things that I did that ended up with my voice getting more and more shagged. And of course, being the sort of new person, I didn't have the authority to kind of say, "You've got to give me two days off. I'm totally exhausted, you know? But, you know, having said all of that, there were some great moments. There were some good shows for me that I enjoyed. I could generally tell during the first two songs how difficult a show it was going to be for me. It was always, you know, Jon was a pretty daunting guy to follow because he's a hell of a singer. I heard some of the board mixes, and I obviously had to study it, and Jon's voice had another minor third on what I've got. My top note was always just a B; it is as high as I can get. You know, when you sing a lot, your top note and your bottom note are what starts to go, you know? That top range… Jon sings an E at the start of "Going For The One." It's amazing, and he's a terrific singer. He's a career singer, you know. I was in a kind of Top 40 band, third-rate singer, just coming into something that was a little more in depth…being realistic…

JK: Chris said, "If Trevor had a fault, and it's not a fault, really, because it was his first big tour, but it was the consistency. I don't think he realised how to pace himself. I think it was in Houston, and I told him after that gig, 'You sang 'And You And I' tonight as well, if not better than Jon Anderson would have sung it.' But there were some nights when he didn't quite hit it, but, you know, that night was certainly a good example of when it was good, it was really good."

TH: No, because, you know, I defy anybody to fucking figure out exactly where to come in with that, (*Sings*) "Coming quickly to terms of all expressions laid," when they're playing some shit, man. It's like singing through an air raid! (*Laughs*)

JK: Well, I always think it's weird when they actually come in because it always catches me out too. I've seen them do it for years and I'm going, "You come in there? Right…" because it's not when you think it's going to come in, which is the weird thing about it.

TH: Steve tried to be helpful. Steve suggested certain massages and stuff… Yes, Chris is right. It was hard for me sometimes because I had no voice, you know. I had very little to work with, and I didn't know how to deal with it. Now, I would know better how to deal with it, but then I didn't, and it's something that I should have done. It's like learning any instrument. But having said all that, there were some nights when I really enjoyed it. I don't know if I was as comfortable with the whole thing at the time, standing up in front of lots of people took me a bit of getting used to, if you know what I mean. Feeling the power of it frightened me a bit, and so it kind of made me tend to stay a bit inwards, you know, because I was trying to keep my head together and get through it, you know?

JK: Were there any songs that the guys, Chris, Steve, and Alan, suggested and you said, "I can't sing that"?

TH: Well, I did "Parallels" once, but I wouldn't do it again because it was just all Bs and it went up to Cs.

JK: It's funny you should say that because Benoit said the same thing when he was in the band.

TH: I just couldn't do it.

JK: Chris said, "Try Parallels," and Benoit said, "Look, you know I'm not Jon Anderson. I can't sing that."

TH: Yes, because it's relentlessly up there, and by the time you've finished it, you're kind of practically on your back.

JK: Of course, it was written for Chris's solo album. It was originally not going to be a Yes song. There just wasn't enough room on *Fish Out Of Water*.

TH: Well, this new guy they've got, Jon Davison, not only is he a lovely guy, but he's a lovely singer, too.

JK: Great singer.

TH: Jon Anderson is Jon Anderson, and ever will be, and he's a hell of a singer. He's like, one of a kind. There's nobody like him, that's for sure. And for me, when it comes to singers in rock, there'd be no two ways about it – Jon Anderson is my favourite singer. I like lots of other singers, too. Robert Plant is an absolutely brilliant singer. He came to a charity deal that I was at about 12 years ago to replace somebody at the last minute. He sang "Knock On Wood," and I thought, *Fuck me, he can even make "Knock On Wood" sound fantastic!*

JK: Yes, but singers like that, people like Robert Plant, are old school so they can do that.

TH: Yes. He has got the chops.

JK: It's when you bring the X Factor sort of element in these days; they don't have that schooling, if you like, of singing in a pub, singing "Mustang Sally" or some Wilson Pickett songs, or Otis Redding songs, and they just don't get to do that now.

TH: Exactly. And, you know, Jon Anderson has got that kind of a voice where I could just listen to him sing for ages, you know? He doesn't have to have much behind him either.

JK: No.

TH: And yet he has still got a voice that will cut through a rock band.

JK: Yes. Absolutely.

TH: You know, that's a hard thing.

JK: Yes… The UK tour was a bit hit and miss. I actually saw two dates, and I thought it was great, but I believe with the London dates, you got a bit of a rough ride, which a lot of bands do, I think.

TH: I think we did a couple of nights at Hammersmith.

JK: And then you did the Rainbow, yes?

TH: And we did the Rainbow. I think the nights at Hammersmith were good. I always remember the best gig being Oxford and enjoying that one the most. But, I didn't think that I wanted to go on with it after the English tour. Although, I had got some material in my head, funnily enough, the stuff that has sort of surfaced on *Fly From Here*. Which, of course, leads one to the kind of amusing thought that it's much better, in a way, that *90125* was the follow-up album to *Drama*, rather than *Fly From Here*, because it's a much better album.

JK: There was a meeting. Geoff said there was a meeting. Was it round at Steve's house or…?

TH: Yes.

JK: And it was decided, then. So, there was definitely a will to carry on. Chris said, "I don't think Trevor was keen…"

TH: I don't think I was. It wasn't working, and my wife really didn't want me to go on. You see, I was kind of… it's hard to do something when you realise that you're only barely good enough to kind of scrape it. I could do the record, but anything else was totally different.

JK: Well, the album was great though.

TH: Yes. And I think by the end of the English tour, I was starting to get a bit of a handle on it, but it was still, you know… you listen to some of those songs, though. Even Jon Davison, you know, rattling through that old "I Am A Camera"… Man, he is so good!

JK: But I actually think *Drama* was a better album than *Tormato* and having heard the story of how that came about, I can see why that would be. There are some nice songs on *Tormato*, but I actually think as an album, Drama is the better album.

TH: Yes. Well, you know, it's more Yes-like, and I suppose – being realistic – Geoffrey and I were very conscious of coming into Yes, and wanting the album to sound like Yes. We got great reviews in the Melody Maker for the New York shows and whatever. Anyway, I think, you know, Geoff definitely got the rock bug, and he could see how, you know, there was a big world out there, you know what I mean?

JK: Well, he told me the first night in Maple Leaf Gardens, he said, "That first show, I just thought then, *I want to do this.*"

TH: Yes, and really, he took to it like a duck to water, but then all that stuff happened, you know? He and I split up because he went off to work with Asia, and I don't blame him for that. I would have done that too because it opened things up for me. I could say to my late wife, "Well, you can manage me now because I don't have a partner." And she said, "Well if I'm going to manage you, forget being an artist. It's not really your thing. You should be a producer because you could be the best producer in the world. That's what you're really good at." So, that's what I started to do, and I forgot about Yes, but I had a couple of things that definitely come from it, right? One was, it made me fearless. Nobody could impress me. I'd fucking done three nights at Madison Square Garden, so you can't muscle me, mate, you know? (*Laughs*)

JK: No.

TH: And I'd been through the fire, right?

JK: Yes, and come through the other side.

TH: And come through the other side. So, even if you listen to the first record my late wife got me to produce, Jill got me to produce, *Hand Held In Black And White*, there's a bit of Yes in it.

JK: "Videotheque" by Dollar, that's another one.

TH: Yes, but like, ding, ding, ding… it was funny, you know? I just banged bits of, you know… I'd been influenced by it. And also, Chris had… I don't know if Chris had shown me something, I don't know; I'd learned something from him about vocal harmonies. But it's one of those things you can't explain, like, there are no rules.

JK: His harmonies are weird. I mean, one I always pull out of the hat is the harmony on "Going For The One."

TH: Yes.

JK: I'm thinking, *What is he singing there?*

TH: What is he actually singing? Yes, for sure; very unique. So, I was a producer for two and a half years, you know, and I still used to see Steve, and I'd still talk to Chris sometimes. I knew what was going on, and then, of course, they started rehearsing. Geoff went off with Asia, had all that huge success, and they were rehearsing in John Henry's, the four of them: Trevor Rabin, Chris, Alan, and Tony Kaye…

JK: Originally Rick Wakeman was pencilled in for the keyboard slot because Trevor Rabin liked Rick's work, and Chris said, "No, you and him won't get on. The personalities you both have will cancel each other out. It just isn't going to happen." He goes, "Well, I really like Rick," and Chris says, "No, I know someone who's better," and that's how Tony came into the picture. But of course, it wasn't Yes at that point. It was Cinema, wasn't it?

TH: It was Cinema, yes.

JK: So, you came in, and you made the approach to produce that, then?

TH: No. Chris was saying, "Come down," and he was playing. I went down and heard him play, and they were playing stuff like "Cinema," you know, and hearing them play that live, wow! I'd had a really good time with ABC, and then I'd been working with Malcolm McLaren, and I'd done really totally different stuff, you know? To come back and hear them playing, it was just the same old thing for me. It's like, Fucking hell! I've never heard anybody do that – what Chris was doing. And Rabin was obviously brilliant on the guitar, and he was a cheerful chap and funny as hell, right? And Tony Kaye…

fine. And then the next thing that happened, my wife was like, doing an old band, you know, she wasn't very keen on it, really. But I was just coming to the end of McLaren, I think. I'd just finished it, and I booked myself a holiday. I'd had a big success with ABC. The album had just been number one and everything, and so I booked myself a house in Malibu. I'd read about that dude Jimmy Webb writing "MacArthur Park" in a beach house in Malibu. So I rented a beach house in Malibu and went over with my daughter and my late wife, and Yes were working in Topanga Canyon at Trevor Rabin's house, and they wanted me to come over and listen to some songs.

So, I went over and listened to some songs, and one of the songs I listened to was "Owner Of A Lonely Heart." The first songs Trevor played me… I didn't know how those songs worked. They weren't my kind of song, really, because they were American rock, and I don't really like American rock. If you look at my whole life, I've never really done an American rock band. It's not what I do. A couple of American rock bands have asked me over the years, but it has never been the right time and the right place. My story about "Owner Of A Lonely Heart" is that Trevor left the tape running, and there'd been some other song, "Moving In," I think it was. "I'm moving my love into you…" some song like that. He went to the toilet, and he left the tape going, and "Owner Of A Lonely Heart" came on. And the first thing I really dug, you know, the intro… Trevor had the intro like that on the demo; sort of like that. Not exactly the same, but he had the jump cut at the front, the jump cut where the rhythm comes in. BANG! I fucking love that, right? That's good. Then the verse… didn't like the verse much, but then the chorus, (*Sings*) "Owner of a lonely heart, de de de…" I said to him when he came out of the toilet, "This is a hit song! This is a big hit song!" And he said, "That's not for Yes. Can't do that with Yes."

JK: Well, Clive Davis had turned that down. He said, "I don't hear that as a hit." And he has got the letter. He has it in the studio on the wall.

TH: Trevor has?

JK: Yes.

TH: Well, I hope Trevor verified what I said because that's… I said that that's a hit record.

JK: Yes. He did. He did say that.

TH: From then on, I liked Cinema, and I really liked that. And I said to my wife, "I'm going to do it. I know it's kind of mad, but…" And she said, "Who's going to be the singer?" I said, "Well, Trevor Rabin." But looking back on it, I was fucking mental to do it, really. I could have done so many other things. I could have made loads of 12-inches. I could have done all kinds of things. But it's always been a bit of an Achilles Heel with me. I can get carried away with music, rather than what I should be doing, because it wasn't easy going from programmed drums and everything to having them play for real. But putting the initial backing tracks down was tricky. It was really tricky. It was trickier than *Drama*, for some reason.

JK: Really?

TH: Yes. Even though we'd worked together before, it was more difficult. And then when we got through everything that we had to put down, I think we started off in the Townhouse, and then we moved out of the Townhouse. And then we went to Air, and we got some great stuff at Air, and we also had some big rows at Air too; Chris being late, and stuff like that. But we got a great drum sound from Alan, even though we didn't use the track. It ended up on the *Art Of Noise* album, you know? (*Laughs*)

JK: Really?

TH: Yes. Alan was the first digital drum loop in the world. It was Alan White.

JK: Got you. Wow. Well, talking about the rows... because I've spoken to Tony Kaye about this period, and he said, "You know, I'd just had enough. I'd had enough of London, and I'd had enough of Yes. Chris originally brought me in saying, 'Look, we want you to do this. We want to go back to the sound of *The Yes Album*,' and it wasn't really like that. I guess he wanted the feel, maybe an underlying feel, rather than an in-your-face feel with the Hammond and all that. But I'd had enough. I'd had an agreement to do the next Badfinger album, so I left."

And then Trevor said, "It was really weird. I went into the studio and Tony's gear wasn't there, and Trevor said, 'Let's go for a walk,' and we were walking around a cemetery and he says, 'You've got to do the keyboards.'" So, whether that's true or not, I don't know, but that was what he told me.

TH: Well, that's a good way of saying that it happened. What happened was, some of the music was really quite complex. I don't know how the fuck it ended up there, but that's the way it ended up. Something like "Changes" in particular...

JK: Yes.

TH: And I was just getting to know Trevor, and one afternoon he said to me, "You know, there could be a really nice piano part on 'Changes.' Let me show you." He sat down at the piano, and he played the most beautiful thing, and I said, "My God. You never told me you played the keyboards." He said, "I was a child prodigy on keyboards. When I was 14, I could play like Rachmaninoff," or whatever. I was like… and I thought about it. I thought, *We've got to sort this out. This music…it needs him to play the keyboards.* And so I sorted it the best way I could, you know. So that happened, and I have to say that Tony was really good about it. He had another record to go to and so he wasn't arsed. And I think he could see what he was going to be in for, and he was probably kind of relieved, so… And then we went through a great two or three months where Trevor and I had the best time because the thing about Trevor is, he has got a great sense of humour. He's dead funny! He's a great imitator, and we just worked every day from like, 1pm through to about 8 in the evening doing keyboards and guitars. And, you know, you could say anything to Trevor. Throw anything at him… he'd do it. You know, if he didn't have an idea, you'd say, "Hey, what about…remember that funny thing on that record there?" And he'd go, "Oh, yes." "Remember that?" "Oh yeah, sing it to me… yes." Trevor could do anything. And on the keyboards we had JJ [Jonathan Jeczalik] getting sounds on the Fairlight, and JJ would come up with a sound and Trevor would do something amazing with it, and then the whole thing sort of started to take off a bit, you know? Alan was brilliant on that record, you know. I mean, I won't go into it, but I'm sure you've heard all the arguments of me falling around on the floor and begging them to play. Let me program "Owner Of A Lonely Heart!"

JK: Yes. I did.

TH: And getting to do it and all the negativity about the way the drums were tuned and all that bollocks…

JK: Yes, I know, but that does happen with a lot of bands and a lot of musicians.

TH: Yes. That's standard.

JK: It is. I've worked with bands for 40 years, so believe you me, I know what that score is. But some of the songs were so un-Yes-like.

TH: Yes. Well, something like "Leave It" was some kind of idea that they had that they sang to me or started. Chris had the "Leave It" bit, I think, you know, and I wrote the verses. I might have even written the lyric for the front, the "Sense of measure" line. It sounds a bit like me, and at that point, we were really getting on great. The only problem we were having really was the lead vocal.

JK: Trevor said, "I really wanted to be the singer. I'd already had this problem with a couple of record labels who wanted to mould me a certain way." One of which was Geffen, and John David Kalodner wanted to put him into Asia. The problem was, they didn't tell Steve Howe he was turning up. He thought of getting a singer in, and he said, "Well, it's my album, I'm Trevor Rabin, I'm signed as a solo artist, so it's going to be me singing these songs." So, it was one of those things, and he said, "A lot of the stuff on *90125* was going to be on the original solo album that I got the deal for first with RCA." Then he got the development deal with Geffen. But then there were a few things worked up that weren't originally going to be on the album. The song "Cinema," I heard that was edited down. It was a lot longer song. The instrumental "Cinema" was part of a lot longer song called "Time." Is that the case?

TH: Yes. When they played it live at my gig, they played the bit that used to follow it, you know, the whole instrumental bit. Yes, I can imagine that some of that material… I think something like "Changes" is a point in case, but I think a lot of it was quite… do you know what? It was a combination of things. How does Trevor feel about that?

JK: Well, Trevor said he was fine, but he also said he was the last holdout when everyone said, "Look, we've got Jon Anderson. It's got to be Yes." He said, "I didn't have a problem with Jon coming in. In fact, I thought it was great! However, I did not want it to be Yes. I definitely did not want it to be Yes."

And Tony Kaye said, "We were all set as Cinema. We were signed as Cinema, and then Jon Anderson came in and sang on some songs, and of course, the record company heard it, saw dollars, saw Yes, and that was it, from that moment, really. It was only ever going to be Yes from that moment the record company heard it. Once Jon came in, that was it. It's Yes."

And Jon said as well, "You know, if I'm singing on it, and Chris is playing on it, and Alan is playing on it, it is Yes really, you know?" I mean, when did he come into the picture?

TH: God, if you weren't writing it in the book, I could tell you how it happened! (*Laughs*) Well, really what it came down to in the end, was a lead voice, a lead person. And Trevor had a great voice, but he didn't feel like he was the lead singer. I don't know. I just couldn't feel it because some of the material was, even if it may have been originally intended for other things or whatever, it did change quite a bit lyrically. When Jon came in, he changed some of the lyrics and whatever, and something like "Leave It" he didn't change because we'd already written that. Trevor could be so funny because one minute he couldn't sing the lead because his voice wasn't right, and then half an hour later, he'd come up with an idea for a harmony and go and sing the most ridiculous high notes, totally confidently and brilliantly. I mean, that singing at the front of "Leave It" with him and Chris… they're about, you know… I four-tracked them or something. It's a great little bit of singing, beautiful, you know?

JK: It is.

TH: The singing on the choruses of ["City Of Love"] "We'll be waiting for the night…" that's Trevor and Chris again. Brilliant! All different, you know; we didn't fly it over. All the phrasing, you know, it took ages to do that. I say ages because we were pretty meticulous about it. Trevor's whole influence on that record, and something like "City Of Love" was such a weird hybrid, because it was so American rock, and yet not quite, and really interesting.

JK: I think the most Yes-like track on that whole album is "Hearts."

TH: "Hearts," yes. Well, I always remember the big argument on "Hearts" was the lyric "Be ye circle." There was a load of talk about "Be ye circle." Jon, you know… the thing was, I thought it could be a really big album. I thought, you know, Trevor and I fought like mad over the verses of "Owner Of A Lonely Heart." We had a lot of arguments, and we fell out, but we always made friends again and started again. We really would shout at each other sometimes, you know, over the fucking lyrics, right? You know, trying to get them so that they were not banal shit, you know? And something like "Owner Of A Lonely Heart" had him and me staying up all night. I didn't use to drink then, but I actually think I had a drink and tried all kinds of things on the verse. And then, at about two in the morning, I came up with, (*Sings*) "Move yourself. You always live your life, never thinking of the future. Prove yourself…" all that stuff. I just came out with it, and I got 15% of the song for it, you know? I wrote the two verses, more or less. I think Trevor had changed the tune a bit, maybe. But anyway, Trevor did the guide vocal because Jon had already sung it. He'd sung Trevor's original verse. Jon wasn't very pleased when he heard it. I always remember we played it to Chris on a Friday and Chris said, "I don't know if it's any better," and then he phoned me on Sunday and said, "I've been thinking about it; that tune is better. We'd better do it with Jon tomorrow." So, we did it. Jon at first didn't want to do it, you know, and told me off. He said, "We're wasting time," and stuff like that. Then he did it.

JK: What were your expectations for the album when you finished it?

TH: What were my expectations?

JK: Yes. How did you think it was going to be received? It was so radically different from anything Yes had done before.

TH: Well, I have to say that then we had a great time mixing the record. Me, Gary [Langan], and Chris, you know… God, I miss him. I mean, Gary and I worked during the day, and Chris would show up ten at night or something. We were so mental with the mixing because – don't forget – we had two recorders. We had a 24-track and a 16-track analogue linked together. All the original tracks were on 16-tracks. That's why the album sounds really good, even to this day, you know? I actually think it set a benchmark for rock records at the time. Even though I'm bragging, it did, because it had shit on it that nobody had ever tried over rock before, and the playing was amazing, and you've got these guys who have been playing stadiums for ten years. Suddenly, you know, the drummer gets a few noises on a sampler. Listen to what he does! Listen to "Leave It." Listen to the middle of "Owner Of A Lonely Heart." That's all Alan fucking around on a sampler, you know? Alan is brilliant on the piano and, you know, the ideas, the harmony ideas, the way they turn the beat round on "Leave It," the way he did all the fills, you know… so Yes-y, but so robotic at the same time. It was great.

And what were my expectations? Well, you know, the mixing process was great until the mixes were sent to America and nobody liked the mixes. Well, I mean, to be specific, Jerry [Jerry Greenberg, Atlantic Records President] didn't like the mixes. That took a few weeks to resolve. And there were a few tears during that… the remix of "Owner Of A Lonely Heart" with the snare drum tuned down a fifth, which is what Jerry had been aching to do. But in the end, Jerry came over, and we finished off the mixing, and then we cut it over here. Trevor did a really good cut of it in America, where he did everything. He knows how, and he made it sound really good for American radio. So, what were my expectations? I played "Owner Of A Lonely Heart" to a couple of people, and I saw the effect it had on them. I had high expectations. I thought, *This is going to fucking blow people away.* This record… because I've never heard a track like that. How the fuck did it come out like that?

JK: And the proof was in the pudding because it was huge everywhere in the world, except the UK. It didn't even make the Top 30 in the UK, which I think is crazy.

TH: I think it got to 28 one week.

JK: Was it?

TH: Yes. Well, I can tell you, the week that it came out in the UK, I bought the NME. I was in New York, and I sat in a café reading the reviews. The review of Yes was this long, a couple of paragraphs, not even that, really. The big star review was a group called Bogshed. I kid you not.

JK: Bogshed?

TH: Bogshed.

JK: I remember them, actually.

TH: The review of Yes was about this big, and basically the first paragraph went like this: "Who can believe these boring old farts are still going? Why don't they fucking top themselves? Having said that, there's a couple of good tracks on this, particularly 'Owner Of A Lonely Heart.' Anyway, they should basically all fuck off and die." You know, that was the review.

JK: That's a nice backward compliment buried in the middle of a two-paragraph review. Well, what Trevor said about that tour was that the seeds of their success were sown in that, but also if you like, their downfall. He said, "We toured it, and the promoters and the record company just saw blood. They worked us." I said, "Well, it was the longest tour you ever did. It was the longest tour Yes ever did." They've never done a tour that long since.

TH: How long?

JK: It was nearly a year.

TH: Yes, but they were so successful.

JK: Well, that's it. And Trevor said, "Well, they just kept adding dates and adding dates, and at the end of it, everyone said, 'Right, next album.' But I had to say, 'I need a break.' Lots of bands can go to the studio and write in the studio. Yes couldn't. The lack of material for *Big Generator* was the problem." And he likened Yes to a whale: "It's like a whale in the sea. In the ocean, it's a beautiful thing. But when it's on the beach, it's not very good at all. And then we had managerial problems." So, what happened with regards to the recording of *Big Generator*? You were in on the start, but you didn't finish it.

TH: Well, what happened with the recording of *Big Generator* was that it was Yes. I suppose, after the huge success of *90125*, it seemed crazy not to do the next album. But there were certain things sort of against it a little bit at the start, and one of them was the difficulty of… I don't know how much of this to say, really. There were a couple of problems. I made a couple of fundamental mistakes. I started out working with an engineer that wasn't the right person, in a strange place for financial reasons. It wasn't necessarily the best place. And then, you know, there were lots of difficulties with Jon and the band figuring out who was in charge. And everybody was a long way apart; I mean, miles apart.

JK: There was a lack of material, and there were no lyrics. They were just instrumental ideas, apart from "Love Will Find A Way," but it was all just dysfunctional. It was one of those things, and I suppose it became obvious after the Atlantic 40th Anniversary concert. It was definitely going to be the last gig for Yes, at that time. And Trevor Rabin commented that when Anderson Bruford Wakeman Howe came out, he thought that was the next logical step for Yes. But he also said that he didn't sort of figure Chris into the equation. Chris wanted to continue as Yes.

TH: And Chris got it back together again, didn't he?

JK: He did, yes. Then they were asked to record the *Union* album, which was great for the fans, but I believe it was not quite the greatest thing for the band. Bill Bruford thought they had a great time doing it live, but at the same time, recording the album was difficult. But then, following the *Union* tour, Phil Carson put Victory together, and he said he wanted the *90125* line-up.

TH: Really?

JK: Yes, which is why Rick and Steve weren't part of the *Talk* album. They said, "Bill, we knew, wasn't going to do anymore, but Rick was keen to do something." In the end, Phil Carson just wanted the *90125* line-up. That was one of the first digitally recorded albums.

TH: So, who sang on that album?

JK: Jon.

TH: Jon… God, I don't remember that.

JK: Yes. Jon sang on that. Jon was in everything up until and including

Magnification.

TH: Right.

JK: Which they did with the orchestra. That was a great tour, but they didn't have a keyboard player. They got a guy called Tom Brislin in. Rick was going to do it, but then he got fed up because he said they were arguing about points on t-shirts. It's always the way. I don't think it's any different with any other band, but of course, the bigger the band, the more problems you've got.

TH: Yes, of course. Then there's *Fly From Here*, which just started off as one track with Chris talking me into it, you know?

JK: Well, the minute I heard they were going to do *Fly From Here*, A) I knew you were going to be involved, and, B) I knew Geoff was also going to be involved. And I'd been saying to Chris for ages, "You need to get Geoff Downes back in." Geoff had been asked a couple of times, but he said no, claiming he was always too busy with Asia. I said to him, "You really need to be back in Yes." So, they got him back in the end.

TH: Well, then what happened was, I was just going to do *Fly From Here*, and I went out to work with them, and they had Oliver Wakeman. And he was okay, but, you know, I was like, "You know, man, if I'm going to do this track… I don't have to do it." I'm doing it because Chris had talked me into it, as usual, and I wanted to see him again. I always liked Steve. Steve showed up at a few key points in my life and was a positive influence. He is a lovely fellow and very generous. The few times I have been up on stage playing an acoustic guitar with him, he was really nice to me about my playing, which is nice, not snooty.

But bringing Geoff back in was key. If I'm going to do this track, we might as well bring Geoff back in because he and I wrote it, and he knows what the keyboard part is, you know? So I don't have to think, right, instead of trying to figure out, is that right? That doesn't seem quite right, that's not quite the right…anyway… Basically, Geoff and I came in, and we did four of our old songs, "Fly From Here"… and then when we were routining "Fly From Here," Geoff was there. I think Oliver might have been there as well. I said, "How about this song?" and played them "Sad Night At The Airfield." I just played it to them and sang it, and everybody liked it, and they said, "Yes, we'll do that one." And then it was, "Well, we've got another one, how about this one?" (*Sings*) "Take a table…" ["Madman At The Screens"] …Yes! It's like five against four. That was hilarious! We had a great time with that, getting everybody's head into it. And then by that point, I was doing the album, and I was doing a couple of theirs, and I said, "There's one more if you want it," and it was "Ride The Tiger." Well, it was called "Riding The Tiger." We just did it, you know. They got it straight away. It hardly took any time.

JK: Well, Chris said it was one of the easier Yes albums to make.

TH: Absolutely. It was.

JK: Were you surprised then, when Geoff stayed, instead of just doing the album?

TH: No, I'm not surprised. Geoff's great. He's just a cool guy as well. So, I figured once everybody hung together, Geoff would probably re-join the band. The thing that took the longest really, was Benoit because he was at a bit of a disadvantage. It's not his native language – English – and so sometimes it was hard to get the sense – to understand the sense – of how you emphasise something. He was a lovely guy, but getting the right perspective was difficult.

JK: Did you actually sing on the album at all? Because I'm hearing stuff and I'm going, "Trevor's singing on this," and Benoit said, "Well, yes, he is. Essentially, it's the *Drama* line-up with me singing. I did sing the songs. There was one song I didn't want to sing, but I sang it in the end. But yes, Trevor is definitely singing. What you're hearing is exactly that, you're right. You're definitely hearing it correctly. Trevor was singing on the album."

TH: It's nearly always Chris and me doing block harmonies in the back, and there's the odd word from me in the lead vocal, but that's what I've been doing this week. I've just re-sung it all. Benoit is still going to be on it in places, but I just thought it might be a cool thing.

JK: So, you've sung all the vocals on the album now?

TH: All the lead vocals.

JK: All the lead vocals... so is that a potential for release at some point, or is this just something you wanted to do for yourself?

TH: Maybe next year.

JK: Which, of course, makes it the second album from the *Drama* line-up of Yes. Well, that'll be good because I know they have some material left over from *Heaven And Earth*, which Chris is on. Geoff said, "We do have two tracks," and Steve said, "Well, there's one track definitely. Geoff has got others. Billy would know about stuff as well." Billy Sherwood is such a great guy.

TH: He's a lovely guy.

JK: He's a lovely guy, and he's doing a great job as well.

TH: He's doing a great job. He's got Chris's vibe a bit as well; the whole thing. He's a good player.

JK: Yes. He is a good player.

TH: And a good singer…

JK: Yes. Well again, it's a huge place to fill, but he wants to do the job. But then again, you see, this is the whole thing. When he was meant to be replacing Jon Anderson, he said that was never the case because he would never allow that. He said there was no way he was going to set himself up for that.

TH: For that one, yes; a difficult position that I know only too well. (*Laughs*)

JK: He said, "I've got a definite no on that," and it's understandable. Again, he's another guy that I knew was going to end up coming back into Yes at some point. And it's funny because Steve always says that too. It's a strange thing, but he said bands are a strange dynamic anyway, half the time.

TH: They are, yes.

JK: As long as you're not at the point of killing someone, there's always the chance to come back, you know?

TH: Yes, exactly.

JK: So, I mean, would you be considering working on a new album with them again, or is that unlikely?

TH: A new album?

JK: Yes, a new studio album.

TH: No. Well, they need somebody young, you know? I've done my time, you know.

JK: I was surprised that they got Roy Thomas Baker in because again, that didn't work out great the first time either, and they ended up getting Billy to finish that off. They said it was a lot to do with time and I'm thinking, *Well,* *you know, there's time and time*, but I was just surprised.

TH: Roy Thomas Baker is a really good recording engineer and a very charming man, but producing Yes is a huge task.

JK: Well, I just remember that he was involved in the Paris sessions.

TH: Yes, but if the band were together and knew what they wanted, Roy Thomas Baker would be perfect. He would do a great job of giving it to them, but they don't know what they want. What can you do?

JK: And yet it's that very not knowing what they want that makes Yes what it is because they always kind of seem to muddle through in the end, don't they?

TH: Yes, but I always had an advantage as a producer because I had been in the band, so I could help write my way out of a problem. Not many producers do that. Some of them do, you know.

JK: Can I ask you why you didn't get up and play with them on the Princess Trust gig? Because I thought, *What a great opportunity!* You introduced them, and it was a really weird hybrid line-up with Trevor Rabin and Steve Howe. It was an odd line-up, I guess, but it was still Yes.

TH: I didn't want to be singing with Yes again. No way

JK: So, how was it then, having just done the two dates on the recent tour? I mean, you're only doing one number, so you know, "I've only got to do the one number, and I'm out, and that's fine. That's probably about as much as I could stand to do." Is that the case?

TH: Well, it was a bit of a shock to the system at first. I've been a record producer for 36 years. I haven't sung up there for a long time. I mean, I have, but in the studio, you know?

JK: Which is how it was when you started with Yes.

TH: So, it's a bit...going onstage and singing...also in this modern era, you know that everything you do is going to be all over the internet. So, I took it seriously. I worked on my voice a bit to make sure that I would at least be okay, you know, and I looked at it, and I was fine, you know?

JK: Well, I was at the sound checks, and they spent nearly an hour deciding over the last 20 seconds at the end of "Time And A Word."

TH: Well, yes…you're not lost in a 12-bar there. You're not doing it, but the thing that gets me about the Albert Hall thing… Steve is rocking in the verses. He's like, kind of doing… it's almost like Wilko Johnson for a second or two. I can feel the whole band just going, you know, and I was enjoying it. And if you look at me when I go, "Yes!" or whatever… Fuck! I hit the note! Thank God for that. I was dreading being flat on that note, but I got it, you know what I mean?

JK: Yeah, it was great.

TH: It was good fun, and we had a good time.

Following the interview, I had lunch with Trevor. We discussed a lot of things off the record, and he asked me if I wanted to hear his version of *Fly From Here.* **This was in May 2016, and he told me he had just finished the vocals that week. The album was eventually released in 2018 as** *Fly From Here – Return Trip.* **It was nice to hear it before anyone else outside the band, some two years before it was released.**

∼

Trevor Rabin: A Quick Word
November 2003

Trevor Rabin first appeared on the British music scene in the late 70s when his first solo album appeared on the Chrysalis Records label. By the time he performed on tour his second solo album *Face To Face* supporting Steve Hillage, he was starting to make inroads into the British music market. His final album for Chrysalis, *Wolf,* in 1980 was a sophisticated, classic rock album, and things looked very bright for this South African musician. However, his career was to take a turn and lead him to a band that he will forever be associated with: Yes. Trevor hooked up with Chris Squire and Alan White, and his career would never be the same again following the release in 1983 of the Yes album, *90125.*

Let's backtrack, however, to before his solo career. Trevor had been the member of a hugely successful rock band in South Africa called Rabbitt. In this short interview, Trevor talks about those early days of his solo career and before he joined Yes.

Jon Kirkman (JK): What was the music scene like in South Africa when Rabbitt first broke through?

Trevor Rabin (TR): Well, it was difficult for Rabbitt because we were trying to do something, which really hadn't been done before in South Africa. A Western-style white ban is playing original music, and really trying to break in the same way that hadn't been done in South Africa before. Most bands were playing clubs, and the gage of success was, you know, what clubs you played, how much money you were making doing it, and you were basically just doing unoriginal music. So a lot of what Rabbitt was doing in South Africa was unchartered waters with regard to, you know, original music, concept albums, even the promotion. The idea of a band going on the road and playing big shows and long comprehensive tours, promotion, TV shows, it was a very different thing for South Africa.

JK: How difficult a decision was it to move to London, considering that Rabbitt was a pretty big concern in South Africa when you left?

TR: Well, it was a little daunting. I was in my early 20s, wasn't quite sure what I wanted to do, hadn't really been out of the country. I'd been to London for four or five days just to have a look, so I really didn't know what I was getting into. And I had recorded, by the time I'd left, I had kind of finished my first album, but it wasn't properly mixed. And I was setting up a record company and trying to do a lot of things, so I was so busy working out what I wanted to do that I guess I didn't really have time to deal with the incredible fear that I was actually in.

JK: Did you have the deal in place for your first studio album before you recorded it, or did that come after you had recorded the album?

TR: Actually, there was no deal in place when I did my album, other than the production company I was working with. I went to MIDEM in the south of France, which is the kind of record company get together beginning of the year, and really went there to look for deals and see what kind of commitments I could get. Got a lot of bites and stuff, but by the time I got to London after being at MIDEM, there was nothing really solid in effect, and it took a bit of time to get that all together.

JK: Of the first two albums, *Face To Face* actually sounds like a band-generated album. Was that the point that you decided to form a band and go out on tour as you did when you supported Steve Hillage?

TR: Not really. *Face To Face* was done in a pretty similar fashion to the way the first solo album was done. And I had just been recording a lot, doing a lot of solo stuff, producing a lot, and I was just ready to go on the road. I'd been itching to play live, and while I'd been playing a lot and really working really hard, I really wanted to get out and play live. So that was really what led to the tour. Plus, the record company wanted me to tour and get me on the road.

JK: Your final album for Chrysalis, *Wolf*, was an incredibly strong album, and yet at the same time, it seemed that the record company dropped the ball a little with the promotion. Did that disappoint you?

TR: The *Wolf* album, to me, was a really inspiring time. It was, for the first time, functioning more as a band than I did on the first two albums with Simon Phillips on drums and Jack Bruce on bass, Manfred playing keyboards, and it was just very exciting. I thought the material was strong, and I was really motivated by that album. As far as the record company goes, I think Chrysalis did a pretty good job on the whole and, you know, it's just the relationship kinda came to an end, but we had a good time. I really liked the people there, so really, I can't say I have any complaints about them.

JK: How good did it feel when "Owner Of A Lonely Heart" did so well, despite the record company chief saying the original version wasn't commercial?

TR: It was quite interesting when I came back from a couple of meetings with record companies who had said, "We feel your voice really has appeal, but we feel the material is really left-field and a little far-reaching for the way the market is right now." And so, it was pretty satisfying at the end when the album came out the way it did and did so well, because I always had a gut instinct that the stuff was strong and had a place.

JK: Was there a temptation to perhaps change the arrangements of some of the Yes songs you performed during your solo tour to make the point that it was Trevor Rabin solo, rather than Trevor Rabin, member of Yes?

TR: Not really. The only real change and the only real difference from the Yes songs I played on the road as compared to how they were played with Yes, the band, the musicians were so strong, and when the level of musicianship is that strong, the people bring their own personality into it. And I think that was really the fundamental difference that was brought to the Yes material.

JK: There is an album called *90124* on the market at the moment, which contains demos of the songs you recorded with Yes. Will there perhaps be a Volume II in the future?

TR: The record company actually came up with the idea for *90124*. I wasn't sure about the idea at first, but once I got into it and thinking about it and the material, I actually had quite a lot of fun putting it together. I think it's probably a one-off. I don't see there being another one.

JK: You seem pretty occupied with soundtrack work at the moment, but will there be another Trevor Rabin rock album, or perhaps tour in the near future?

TR: Yeah, I've been so busy doing film work that I just haven't had a chance to really focus enough time onto that. But I have been writing, you know, in the last five years or so, and I've got material that I'm really excited about. It's just a matter of putting it all together and just grabbing some time to do it. But as far as actually doing it, I'm absolutely gonna do it, and I'm really hoping I can do it this year.

Following the end of the ARW tour, Trevor returned to his film soundtrack work and (hopefully) work on a new rock album. He has also not ruled out working with Jon Anderson and Rick Wakeman again in the future.

≈

Trevor Rabin: Cinema To Talk
October 2012

Trevor Rabin was born in South Africa, and it was in South Africa that Trevor first enjoyed success as a musician. In the mid-70s, Trevor was a member of one of the biggest pop/rock bands in South Africa, Rabbitt. With Rabbitt, Trevor recorded two hit albums and also enjoyed success with singles. By 1977, he felt he had gone as far as he could with the band and departed for a solo career. His first album was called *Beginnings* and was released in South Africa in 1977. By 1978, Trevor had relocated to London and secured a deal with Chrysalis Records. They released the *Beginnings* album under the title *Trevor Rabin* with a re-sequenced track listing. This was the first of three albums with the label, the other two being *Face To Face* (1979) and *Wolf* (1980). In 1979, Trevor toured in support of the *Face To Face* album, which saw him performing the length and breadth of the UK as the support act to Steve Hillage.

Following Trevor's third album *Wolf*, he left Chrysalis Records and began to look for a new deal as a solo artist. Through a connection with Manfred Mann (for whom Trevor was producing), Trevor got the offer of a deal with Geffen Records. There was a catch, however, as Geffen wanted Trevor to front either a super band, (which would have featured Simon Phillips, John Wetton, and Rick Wakeman) or another band already in existence. The other band was Asia, which Trevor actually got around to rehearsing with. During this time, Trevor wrote the material that would appear on the Yes album *90125*. Trevor was still interested in releasing the album as a solo album, and while RCA was interested, Arista turned him down. One must bear in mind that this album included the future number-one hit single, "Owner Of A Lonely Heart."

Atlantic Records were also interested, and Atlantic's executive suggested that Trevor contact Chris Squire and Alan White. Following what has been described by both Trevor and Chris Squire as the worse jam ever, the trio decided that they liked each other enough to explore the possibility of working together, and the band Cinema was born. As history has proven, Tony Kaye joined the band as a keyboardist, although another important Yes keyboard player could have joined. Once Jon Anderson heard the tapes of the finished album – and in Tony Kaye's words, "Freaked!" – he decided he wanted in on the new band. He was invited to join, and again as history states, Yes was reborn. Trevor would go on to record four studio albums with Yes and spend almost twelve years recording and touring as a member of Yes. Following the tour to promote the *Talk* album, he decided to leave the band and embark on new musical projects, which included writing the music for a number of highly successful films and television programmes. In late 2012, Trevor Rabin was still writing music for films and had just released his most recent solo album *Jacaranda*.

Jon Kirkman (JK): Your solo career in the late 70s came off the back of your career with Rabbitt in South Africa, which was incredibly successful there. However, I seemed to lose track of you after *Wolf* and didn't pick up with you again until *90125*. But a lot happened in-between, including an aborted solo deal, and I believe you also auditioned for Asia. What happened there?

Trevor Rabin (TR): Well, the whole Asia thing was very peculiar because I was producing Manfred Mann in England. Cutting a long story short, David Geffen was speaking to Manfred about possibly releasing the next Earthband album in America. And although nothing came of that, I met David and spent some time with him, and he asked me to come to America on a development deal with Geffen Records. I had done three albums on Chrysalis, and Chrysalis had been fantastic, but the albums didn't sell, sadly. Still, it was definitely a good time for me.

So basically, in the following six months, I was on the development contract. I wrote what was to become the Yes album *90125*, and I wanted to do it as a solo album, but Geffen was reluctant to do that. They wanted me to get together with a band and put what they described as "some big name people" around me. To that end, I had some meetings with Carl Palmer, who came to America, and we hung out a lot together. John Wetton came and rehearsed with the band I had put together in LA, and I got on really well with John. At the time, Simon Phillips was the drummer they were thinking of before they got Carl. I had obviously worked with Simon and got on well with him on the *Wolf* album. So this band was in the back of their mind all the time. So at a subsequent meeting with Brian Lane and David Geffen in London, it was to be this new band with Rick Wakeman, John Wetton, Carl Palmer, and myself. Well we had dinner, and I can't exactly remember what happened, but not much. So I came back to LA and kept on writing, and John Kalodner, who was Geffen's A&R guy said, "Listen, we really want you to join this band with the music you have written." And I said, "Well, I really want to do a solo album," and they basically said, "You have to join this band, or we are going to drop you." I'm paraphrasing here, but basically that is what happened. Now, my manager basically said I should go and do it and at least go through the motions. So I went to London and spent some time, a day or two, I can't remember now, but it wasn't long and played with them. It was pretty forgettable at the time. I remember we played "Heat Of The Moment" and we played a couple of my songs.

JK: So, who was actually in Asia at that point? Was it the recognised line-up of John Wetton, Carl Palmer, Steve Howe, and Geoff Downes?

TR: Yeah, at that point, that is exactly what it was. It's funny really, because John Kalodner said, "Steve Howe is in the mix," and I said, "What do you need me for? You've got a guitarist," and John said, "Oh, you can work together." I said, "No, our styles are completely different, and it wouldn't work," and I'm sure it was not something Steve desired. It was certainly not something I desired.

JK: I think it is pretty much on record that Steve is not a fan of being in a band with another guitarist. That is not a criticism of Steve, just that he considers himself to be THE guitarist in the group. It does seem odd that they would suggest that, so perhaps they thought that you would be the writer in the band.

TR: Well, maybe. That was what Steve was told, but I was certainly told that there was going to be two guitarists. So it was a bit of a shock, I think, to Steve when my gear arrived. He's got one little Fender Twin Reverb sitting there, and suddenly there's this barrage of 200 watt Marshall stacks that's arrived and bearing over his little rig, you know. It wasn't really a pleasant experience, but I had no interest in it, so I came back to LA. And of course, Geffen dropped me, so I just thought, *Okay. I will just send the album round a bunch of people and do a solo album*, and I was very excited about that! It went to RCA Records, and it went to Atlantic. Clive Davis turned down the album, but Ron Fair at RCA was very keen on the album as a solo record, and Atlantic was very keen as well. Neither of them talked bands, as I think they knew what I had just been through, but Atlantic suggested I meet Chris Squire. They said, "If you need a rhythm section, Alan and Chris are looking to do something." So Chris had the material, and we met up, and that was it. We got on really well.

JK: Were you aware that Chris and Alan had just come out of a potential situation with Jimmy Page?

TR: No, I wasn't aware of that at the time, but a little later I was at Chris Squire's studio, and the engineer played me some stuff and said, "Chris is going to be late today, and he wanted me to play you this and see if you want to mess around with it." I listened to it and said, "That sounds like Jimmy Page on here," and the engineer said, "Yeah, just play along with it," but I said, "No, it's done." But I did hear the stuff.

JK: I think some of that ended up on the second Firm album a few years later.

TR: Oh, okay. I didn't know that.

JK: When did Phil Carson come into the picture then? Was the band actually together as Cinema at that point, or was it earlier? I heard you guys did this jam, which according to Chris Squire, was the worst jam ever, but you all got on great.

TR: That was exactly right! (*Laughs*)

JK: So did Phil Carson come in when you were the three-piece? Did he bring or suggest Tony Kaye as well?

TR: Oh, he was in from the start. Chris actually recommended Tony Kaye because he thought Rick Wakeman and I would not get on because we were both headstrong and had strong musical ideas. Tony was a very good guy, "one of the boys" type guy, which is ironic because Rick and I enjoy playing together as well as anyone I have played with.

JK: So, what you are saying is, due to Chris thinking there would be a mismatch between you and Rick, and you and Rick wouldn't have got on, that there was a missed opportunity. Rick could have been the keyboard player in Yes for the *90125* album.

TR: Oh, very much so, yeah. It is weird because Trevor Horn and Tony Kaye didn't get on very well, and I remember coming to the studio one day and Tony Kaye wasn't there. Trevor said, "I need to have a talk with you." I remember it well. We were in the east end of London, and Trevor took me out for a walk. We ended up walking through an old cemetery, and Trevor Horn said, "How do you feel about playing keyboards on the album?" Basically what happened was Trevor and him didn't get on, and we didn't think of any repercussions of what may happen, so I ended up playing the keyboards on the album. It was quite funny because we were thinking, *Well, Tony's not in the band anymore*. Nobody said anything, so it was a kind of weird situation. So when I went back to LA, I rang Tony up and said, "I know you didn't get on with Trevor Horn and things didn't work out, but come and do the tour."

JK: In fairness to Tony, I suppose it is difficult if you don't get on with the producer.

TR: Yeah, yeah.

JK: Being a producer yourself, how do you feel working with another producer? Are you able to do that? It must be difficult taking direction from someone, but again, if you hire a producer and you want to produce, it is a bit like having a dog and barking yourself, isn't it?

TR: Well, I've become much less belligerent now, but at the time my attitude was: "well, I don't like working with a producer either, but they're my songs; live with it" kind of thing, you know? (*Laughs*)

JK: Tony told me that the album was finished and Atco was going to release it as the debut album by Cinema. Then all of a sudden, Chris plays some of the songs to Jon, who was knocked out by the songs he heard, and as Tony said, "Jon freaked and wants to sing on the album." So how did all that come about?

TR: Well, it was funny because on the one hand, it was an incredible compliment from Jon Anderson, and on the other hand, I was being fired as the singer! (*Laughs*) Once Jon came in, and we started working on it, that's when it became quite a peculiar album. A lot of the lead vocals I had done remained on the album because the keys were not necessarily the right key for Jon. So Jon would say things like, "I really like that part so keep that, and I'll come in on the chorus or the verse or whatever it might be." For example, in "Owner Of A Lonely Heart" we kept the lead vocal of mine in the chorus, and Jon sang the verse, so it actually turned out to be a useful and a creative thing. But once I heard Jon singing on a couple of tracks, I was completely hooked.

JK: Were you surprised by just how good the vocal mix of you, Jon, and Chris sounded? It is an amazing mix!

TR: Yeah, the harmony mix between Jon, Chris, and I was about the happiest I have ever been on any mix I have ever done.

JK: Was there any pressure from the record company to bring a singer into the band? Was that why Jon was approached or was it something that just happened?

TR: No, it was really just something that happened. I was going to be the singer, and we were very much excited by that. There wasn't any kind of vibe like, "Oh, I don't know what is happening," unless there is something I don't know about! (*Laughs*) It seemed all very good. It's just that when Jon heard it and gave a great response to hearing it, it was an added kind of bonus. And then once he sang on it, it was, "Oh my goodness!" He really added some stuff to it.

JK: Of course, the album re-launched Yes. How did you feel about it becoming Yes? There is the famous quote of Jon's where he said to Chris, "If I sing on this, it is going to sound like Yes." So how did you feel, having gone through the whole project as Cinema and Tony Kaye said the album was finished? How did you feel about it becoming Yes?

TR: Well, it wasn't quite finished; it was getting there. Certainly the idea of the album was formulated and getting to the end, but it was Cinema. I had no desire to be joining some old rock band, so I was really against the idea of calling it Yes for quite some time. But then there were all kinds of benefits mentioned to me, like going on the road, but I said, "Well, if calling it Yes means going on the road and playing to ten thousand people rather than five thousand people, I would still rather call it Cinema," but they said, "Well, it's more than that. It's getting a stage designer, and getting a stage set would be very much easier because your upfront investment would be increased." And that kind of appealed to me because I was really into having a great lighting system with choreographed lights and some production value.

With Rabbitt I had that, and with the Steve Hillage tour, I had no production at all, and I kind of missed it. So, knowing that would be part of the Yes thing, and after a lot of badgering from Chris and Jon and Phil Carson and Ahmet Ertegun as well – I remember him calling me! (*Laughs*) He was great, though. He said, "You've got a hit song here; it's undeniable. You have this platform, so why not complete the circle?" So reluctantly, I went along with it. In some ways, I'm still sorry it was called Yes.

JK: Well, I have been a Yes fan for more than 40 years, and I had seen Yes on the *Drama* tour, and I liked the *Drama* album. I didn't like the album before that, *Tormato*, and I don't think I am alone there; I think a lot of Yes fans have a problem with that album. But when I heard *90125*, my jaw hit the ground, and the first thing I said was, "This is Yes?" It wasn't that I didn't like it, because I loved it, but it was like a completely different band. But surely that is a good thing!

TR: That's right, and I loved that about it, but I still feel calling it Cinema would have been fine.

JK: Tony had dropped out of the line-up and Eddie Jobson, who is a great keyboard player, came in. He was on the video for "Owner Of A Lonely Heart," and I think one promotional photograph. As much as I think he is a great keyboard player, I never thought he was the right keyboard player for Yes. Did he actually stick around and play on the album at all or even rehearse with the band? Or was he just in for the photo and the video?

TR: No, we had a very short rehearsal, and we started doing the video, but I think it was a case of everything moving so quickly and it was like, "You need someone in the video, and you need someone for the road. Let's try Eddie out." So we had one small rehearsal, and I don't even remember what it was like, but after the video, we got back with Tony, and that was it.

JK: Before the tour kicked off, you were involved in an accident, which turned out to be quite nasty, not to mention an inconvenience for you personally. Here you are with a hit album and a tour ready to go, and you are suddenly side-lined, which must have been distressing for you to say the least.

TR: Well, it was a really peculiar thing. I was on my way up to Lititz in Pennsylvania for rehearsal, and my wife and I decided we were going to go via Miami and have two or three days there or a week. I can't remember exactly what it was, just to celebrate the end of the album and my birthday, which is the 13th of January. So, we arrived on the 11th, and there were no cell phones then, and my manager had said, "When you get to Miami just call me from the airport, and I can give you the chart positions." So I said, "Okay" and I called him. He was very excited and said, "'Owner Of A Lonely Heart' is number-one all over the world, not least in America, and the album is in the Top 5! So go and enjoy yourself!" So we went to the hotel, and I was in the swimming pool having a glass of champagne, and there was this waterfall in the pool, and the waterfall hid the mouth of a cave, and out of this cave came a slide and this woman came down the slide and went full bore into my stomach. She weighed about 200lbs, and she ruptured my spleen. So I was in the hospital under observation on the 12th and on the 13th, my birthday, I had an operation to remove my spleen.

JK: How soon were you expected to go on tour?

TR: Well, they had to cancel the tour as I was in recovery for six weeks, and there was the talk of litigation and such. But yeah, it was a little distressing.

JK: You have said that "Owner Of A Lonely Heart" was number-one all over the world, but before you hooked up with Yes, I believe one of the record company executives said, "I don't hear a hit single here," which must have made the news that it got to number-one all the sweeter.

TR: In fact, that was when I was looking for a solo deal, and I have a letter from Arista, Clive Davis' company, and the letter says: "While we feel your voice has Top 40 appeal, we don't feel the songs…" and then they have them listed in brackets, "Changes," "City Of Love," "Owner Of A Lonely Heart," "… We don't feel they have the hit potential that is needed in the marketplace today. We feel it's far too left field."

JK: I imagine you could have heard the grinding of Clive Davis' teeth from this side of the Atlantic when "Owner Of A Lonely Heart" got to number one.

TR: Well, you know, he did the *Union* album, and we were backstage at Madison Square Garden, and he was talking to me. I had sat with him for hours when we were mixing "Lift Me Up," and so many times I wanted to say, "You know, you turned down a pretty big record…" He's obviously forgotten about it, but I could always show him the letter! (*Laughs*) I think I should frame it and put it up in the studio!

JK: You should, yeah! Make it pride of place, or maybe do a copy and let the Hard Rock Café have it!

TR: (*Laughs*) Exactly, yeah! That's a good idea.

JK: Let's look at the live angle, then. The tour to promote *90125* was an incredible tour, and I researched this so I could get it right. It was 160 dates over a twelve-month period, and looking at subsequent tours, I don't think Yes ever went out for that long again. And in actual fact, I don't think they ever toured that much prior to *90125* either. That must have been both gruelling and fantastic all at the same time.

TR: Yeah, I guess I was by far the youngest in the band, so the gruelling side didn't really hit me back then, but I am sure it would today. It was definitely over the top for sure. It was saliva dripping out of the promoters' mouths along with probably a bit of blood! (*Laughs*)

JK: With the tour being so big, the only thing that surprised me was that there wasn't a live album. There was a live video and a mini live album, *9012Live: The Solos* with some tracks drawn from the video, but no full album. Is there some regret that you didn't capture the show on a double live album along the lines of *Yessongs* or *Yesshows*? I think it was a bit of a missed opportunity, personally speaking.

TR: Yeah, you're right. If there was time and we could locate where the tapes were, I know there were a couple of analogue two-inch tape machines linked together to record some of the shows. It's not like it's not there; it could be done. There's a couple of things like that, really. One of the things that is a regret for me is that I did a tour for my album *Can't Look Away,* and there is a live album because we recorded some of the shows and the band was playing really well, and I am just sorry there isn't a video of that.

JK: I'm thinking, of course, from a business point of view, that live albums are notoriously used as bargaining chips and contractual fillers, so I'm quite surprised that the management didn't think along those lines as well.

TR: You know, I think possibly the reason with Yes and why it didn't become an issue, is because there was never the thing where we had to deliver six albums or whatever to fulfil the contract in a certain period. Plus, the band was in such a state of disarray at the time. No one knew who was in the band or going to be in the band from one day to the next.

JK: That does seem to have been the story of Yes for some time, and you can probably see this now from the outside as well, but there has been so much coming and going with Yes that has been down to not just musical differences, but also management. I think in the past, Yes could have done with stronger management at various points in their career. I think because of this, the band has missed out on some really important opportunities.

TR: I think you're right. It was Tony Dimitriades at the time. He has done a phenomenal job with Tom Petty, and he managed to get us on the road, but he had so many other issues to deal with for Yes though. I will say we must have been a nightmare band to manage.

JK: And you were in it! (*Laughs*)

TR: (*Laughs*) Yeah, I was in it! I have to be honest!

JK: It was a twelve-month tour, give or take. So how long after the tour did work begin on *Big Generator*? Tony Kaye has said he just needed to get away and take time off. He thought the other guys in the band needed to take time off too, as there wasn't time to draw breath really over the twelve-months, as it was so gruelling.

TR: I think he is right. I think we went into *Big Generator* and it became a really laborious and hard project, and halfway through we parted with Trevor Horn. Luckily, Paul De Villiers came in and was a real big helping hand. And then at the end, I think I spent nine weeks mixing it or something, so it was really a hard and tough project.

JK: Why did Trevor Horn leave the project? Was it just dissent within the band or dissent between him and the band? On the outside, it made perfect sense for him to produce the follow up to *90125*.

TR: Well, I wouldn't even blame Trevor Horn for anything, much. I think the band was just going through what it usually goes through, in that it was untogether. Yes is like a beached whale. It's really not attractive, but if you can somehow push it out into the ocean, it's wonderful when it's swimming, but the problem is that it always seems to be on the beach.

JK: Well, as a fan, I can understand what you are saying. They celebrate their 45th Anniversary in 2013, and there can be an awful lot of frustration in there from a fan's point of view. But I am sure it must be frustrating for members of the band at times as well; it does seem to be very stop-start at times.

TR: Yeah, yeah. I have to be honest, there were times I'd get really pissed off with various things, and Tony Dimitriades used to come to me a lot from a political standpoint to say, "Look, here's the logic. We need to do this." And he'd try to get me to do this or that, and I would, but I don't know if it was because I was younger than the other guys or what, but it really didn't bother me much; all the crap that went on, you know.

JK: From a creative point, then, what was it like in terms of material? Did you have much material for *Big Generator*?

TR: No! Well, that was the big difference. With *90125*, all the stuff was pretty much written, so we had the luxury of going in and trying other new things like "It Can Happen," knowing that we had this really good foundation of songs like "Hearts," "Changes," "Owner Of A Lonely Heart," "City Of Love," and "Hold On" And there were some nice accidents as well. For example, "Our Song" was something that happened in rehearsal. It was actually written during the rehearsals for *90125*, but most of it was demoed, and I even put out an album after called *90124*, which was all the demos for *90125* and *Big Generator*.

JK: Could you not perhaps reach back to some of the older songs to beef it up? There are some great songs on *Big Generator* like "Love Will Find A Way," "Rhythm Of Love," and "Shoot High Aim Low," and for me, they are every bit as good as some of the songs on *90125*.

TR: Absolutely! And you have just mentioned my three, by far, favourite songs on the album.

JK: How was the situation with Stevie Nicks, then? She is on record saying that you wrote "Love Will Find A Way" for her, rather than Yes.

TR: Yeah, you are right. Tony Dimitriades did call me and said, "Stevie Nicks is looking for a song," and I did go out and very specifically write "Love Will Find A Way" for Stevie. And then when the album started, Chris heard it and played it to Trevor Horn who said, "This is the 'Owner Of A Lonely Heart' of this record!" I always thought it could be a single, but I thought of it more as a second single, rather than the lead single from the album. But I think it was the first single from the album.

JK: The other great track was "Shoot High Aim Low," which did get an incredible amount of airplay on American radio.

TR: Yeah, it did. I don't know if you have heard many of the live bootlegs from the tour – most are dreadful – but there are a couple of good ones, and some of the versions have a little extra something on them.

JK: Was that the big showcase track from that album for you?

TR: Well, for me, it was definitely. And I think, to a lesser degree, although he would be happy to say it, I think Jon would say that is the best track on the album. In fact, I think everyone would. But for me, I think it was clearer than it was to other people.

JK: The subsequent tour for *Big Generator* was very much pared down from the 160 dates for the *90125* tour. It was 70+ dates over five months, so you weren't even out on tour for half the time you were for *90125*. Can I ask you, were there problems within the band at this point? Shortly after the concert to celebrate the Atlantic Records 40th Anniversary, Jon left the band again, so was it really that bad, or was it manageable?

TR: No, really, it got way worse. It was pretty unmanageable. Chris and Jon weren't getting on, Chris was partying a lot, and to be honest, I'd not lost interest. It was such a hard album for me to finish.

JK: Well, nine weeks to mix an album does seem like a very long time to mix an album.

TR: Yeah. Well, you're mixing problems a lot of the time. And then the tour was about to start, and Jon had an idea for production, which cost us a small fortune, and then we didn't use it. Then halfway through the tour, we had to get a different lighting system and changed the lighting people. Someone else came in, so it was really a huge mess in all ways. From management to band, to you name it; it was really a bit of a mess, and the writing was on the wall. It couldn't have continued like that, and in retrospect, maybe we should have seen that coming, because the way that *90125* was built was on a very solid foundation of songs. With *Big Generator*, we went into the studio, and we didn't really have any songs. The thinking was, we would write them as we go along; that sometimes works, but it certainly wasn't going to work on this one.

JK: It is strange really because that is almost how the break with Jon and Rick came after trying to record the follow up to *Tormato*. I think they got bogged down and maybe lost interest then. So I am not altogether convinced that Yes should go into the studio and work that way.

TR: No, it's not, and in this instance, wasn't. As far as the glass half full scenario is concerned, I was quite excited by things like "Rhythm Of Love," "Shoot High Aim Low," and "Love Will Find A Way." And I thought as far as the band playing together, "I'm Running" was pretty good. But when we started to try and play it live, Jon couldn't remember the parts, and we played it one night, and it was awful. So rather than spend time trying to get it right, it was just dropped from the set. So, even though some dates were really good, the writing was on the wall.

JK: When I look at the tour dates and the setlist, you actually performed every track from *Big Generator* at some point during the tour. Do you think that maybe that is just a little too much with a new album? Perhaps you could have done a typical Yes set with maybe just the three songs we have mentioned, and perhaps that would have made for a better set.

TR: Yeah, possibly. In fact, if you look back to what we did with *90125*, because it was such a big album, we were able to do every song, and everyone knew every song. Whereas with *Big Generator*, it wasn't that kind of album. It wasn't as deep with regards to audience recognition, so yeah, going in and doing that was wrong.

JK: Presumably then, you weren't surprised when Jon left following the Atlantic show. But were you surprised when he teamed up with Bill Bruford, Rick Wakeman, and Steve Howe?

TR: Well, if I'm honest, at the time, I just thought it was inevitable after *Big Generator*. I really didn't mind as I was very set on doing a solo album at the time, and wanted to concentrate on that. I also wanted to spend some time writing with Roger Hodgson, who had been trying to get a hold of me for a time, and actually drove out here from Nevada City near Sacramento. So we spent a long time writing together, both here and up at his studio, and one of the tracks that came from those sessions was "Walls," which, as you know, ended up on the *Talk* album.

JK: Can I ask you then, when you did *Can't Look Away*, which was the solo album you just mentioned, was everything on that album written for that album, or were there any songs that could have been recorded by Yes?

TR: No, it was all written for that album, but I absolutely feel that some of the songs could have been done by Yes. It could have helped Yes on the *Big Generator* album, but the timing was out and all different, really.

JK: You went out and played a few solo dates in promotion of the album, which I believe your management did not want you to do.

TR: They didn't want me to do it, and the record company really wanted me to do it. The song "Something To Hold On To" was nominated for a Grammy. It was a number-one AOR track on the radio, so it was one thing that I think the management got a little bit wrong. The tour could have been a little bit longer, or I could have got a support on a bill with a big band or something, but it never happened. But I did record a live album from the tour because the band were just right.

JK: How did it feel going out with your own band? Was there a sense of relief after the problems of *Big Generator* and being outside the Yes bubble, so to speak?

TR: Oh, it was glorious. I absolutely loved it! The players I got were just phenomenal players. They never missed a trick and were great to play with.

JK: What was it like then, when you got the call to go back to Yes? I'm specifically talking about the period between *Big Generator* and the *Union* period. I know Billy Sherwood came into the orbit of Yes during this period, and there is a song called "Love Conquers All." Then there are the stories that Roger Hodgson and Billy Sherwood were considered to fill the role vacated by Jon. Is there any truth to these stories?

TR: Yeah, definitely with Roger. I got Chris and Alan to come up to Nevada City to have a jam with Roger with a view to that, but we never got to the point where it was really considered. As for Billy Sherwood, he was doing a side project with Chris, so I don't think that was ever a consideration. Although, they did write the song, as you say, "Love Conquers All," and I ended up singing that on the boxed set.

JK: When I spoke to Billy, he said he wasn't keen on replacing Jon Anderson. After all, they were big shoes to fill!

TR: Yeah, they are, but I was in the band at the time, and I knew what was going on. I don't recall Billy being asked to join the band to replace Jon, because my view (outside of someone like Roger Hodgson) was, "Don't do it. Go and do something else, rather than make an album without Jon Anderson." That was always my view and remains that way. The only way Billy was considered was because there was a time on tour when Chris had some health issues. We couldn't get insurance, and the only way we could get insurance would be if we had a stand-in. So, if Chris was sick and couldn't play that night, we would have a stand-in. So Billy learned the set and was going to be the stand-in bass player. After about fifteen gigs, we had Billy standing on the side of the stage, and apart from it being a bit macabre, we thought, *Well, why don't we have him playing some guitar or doing backing vocals?* So, that is how he came to be involved, particularly on the *Talk* tour. I think once again after the tour, when Yes broke up, Billy had a little studio in the Valley and Yes were looking for somewhere to record, so that is his involvement there. Since he was a huge fan of Yes, he really understood the band.

JK: Over the years, the Yes fan base has been divided about the *Union* album and even some of the members of Yes as well. And even though there are eight members of Yes on the album, it still arouses such controversy.

TR: Well, let me tell you how that album came about. Anderson Bruford Wakeman and Howe were doing another album. Out of the blue, I get a call from Jon, and he leaves a message along the lines of: "Oh if you've got any good songs, we're looking for songs for ABWH." So I had "Lift Me Up," which I thought was a Yes-y type of song. So I called Clive Davis and said, "I've just had a call from Jon. What's happening?" And Clive said, "Yeah, we need a single. There are no singles on the record, and it's not what it needs to be, so if you've got a bunch of songs, what we especially need is a hit single and some other material." So I said, "Well, I've got a song, but I don't really want to give it to Anderson Bruford Wakeman and Howe because it's something I want to do myself. It's not something like 'Love Will Find A Way,' because I do still feel a bit guilty about that because I did write that for Stevie, but 'Lift Me Up' was something I wrote for myself." So Clive heard the song because I sent it to him anyway, and he said, "This is the single. All we have to do is somehow put it together." And that is when I think the idea came about.

Steve Howe was apparently unhappy with the ABWH thing because the producer had replaced a lot of his parts and it was apparently not a happy place, the ABWH album sessions. But I said, "Well, I'm not touching that, [The ABWH album] but what I am prepared to do is record a couple of tracks with the 'Yes-West' band because I had recorded these things." I got Chris in, and he played bass on it. Then Alan came in and played on it, and then Jon came and sang on it. We did "Lift Me Up," "Miracle Of Life," and "Saving My Heart," which was once again not meant to be a Yes song, but we did those three songs and kind of threw them together with the Anderson Bruford Wakeman Howe stuff. I think Chris went and played or sang on some of those tracks to legitimise it. It was really not a Yes album, but it was put out as one.

JK: I think the big complaint – and this is even from Rick Wakeman – is that there are too many people on it. I had a look at the credits, and there are about ten people credited as playing synthesizers on the album, which seems a little over the top.

TR: I know, it's crazy.

JK: Do you think it might be better if, at some point in the future, the master tapes could be found and maybe it could be stripped back to the real performances? I feel that underneath all that is a reasonable album. When I hear songs like "Shock To The System," which is an ABWH song, I was very surprised because it does sound like a "Yes-West" song.

TR: Yeah, I think Steve had a lot to do with that song. I think he was number painting with "City Of Love."

JK: But do you feel, as an album, it could be better if perhaps someone could go in and strip it back to the original "Yes" performances, away from the session tracks? I'm not saying it would be like saving a masterpiece, but I think it would benefit from removing the session tracks away. Would you perhaps agree with that?

TR: Well, I don't know the producer, Jonathan Elias, but I do know people who do know him, and he is a person who deserves respect. And I think you have to also look at what he was dealing with. I think he would have been the happiest guy alive if they had come in and played something that was good, so something obviously happened where he wasn't happy. I wasn't privy to it or what happened. I have no idea what happened really, but the great thing about *Union* is that I don't have to know anything more about *Union* than I know.

JK: It just seems to me that of all the Yes albums, *Union* is the album that has the least amount of input from Yes, in a way.

TR: Yeah, but in the case of the songs that I was involved in, there were no foreign bodies on it. It was all people from Yes! (*Laughs*)

JK: How did you feel about going on tour with the eight-man Yes, then? It was a many-legged and armed monster, wasn't it?

TR: Well, I was kind of interested, in some ways, but let's be honest – it was clearly something that was put together by businessmen! (*Laughs*)

JK: Everyone I have spoken to has said exactly the same thing.

TR: Yeah, well, let's be honest – Steve and I have no desire to be playing together, but the one thing that happened that was fortunate was that my relationship with Rick was very strong.

JK: Oddly enough, following the *Union* tour, there was going to be another album made, and Rick was originally meant to be a part of the line-up that would go on to record what would become *Talk*. So, were you disappointed when Rick had to drop out?

TR: I think when it came to *Talk*, and the deal was done with this Japanese record company, Victory Music, because of the fiasco that was *Union* with the eight-piece thing, I was happy to work with Rick. But I think an album with Steve and I would have been pointless because, as you have rightly said, Steve is a guitarist who likes to be THE guitarist in a band. While I am happy to work with other people who want to work with me and are capable of working with others, I don't think Steve is, in terms of other guitar players.

JK: Which is no reflection on Steve, because there are a lot of guitarists out there who are like that.

TR: Oh no, this is no reflection on him at all. But for me, it was just a matter of, "Let's get back to doing this for the right reasons and stop all this nonsense of doing something like *Union*, which was clearly contrived."

JK: Watching the video of the *Union* tour, there did seem to be at least some good times. It was exciting because at times it did seem like you, Steve, Bill, Alan, Tony, and Rick were all enjoying yourselves.

TR: I think there were times when that thing took off, and it was way larger than the components. It became something where it seemed that there weren't eight people on stage, but a thousand people on stage. So, I have to admit that there were times when the sum of the parts added up to something really special, and none of us would ever have been able to put our finger on it and said, "This is how you do this."

JK: When you came to the *Talk* album, you recorded it digitally. Was this the first album you had recorded digitally?

TR: Well, yes and no. *Big Generator* was done on a Linear Dash System [Dash is a reel-to-reel digital recording method], and I have always been into technology, I've always had a studio, and I was absolutely hell-bent on recording a non-linear computer-based album. I must say, we did record a lot of it in analogue and then transferred it to digital, but it was such early days of digital. You could only have four tracks per computer, so it was really the early stages of digital recording. I actually had a technician from MOTU, Mark Of The Unicorn, the digital company, sitting next to me taking notes on what we could and couldn't do. He would be on the phone to Boston (where the company's HQ was) every night, telling them to re-write the codes so I could be ready to do stuff the next day. So, it was really a kind of frontier thing. I ended up linking four machines together in order to do it.

JK: So, in effect, *Talk* was the digital equivalent of *Sergeant Pepper*.

TR: Yeah, it really is. It was the first time that had been done. I'm kind of glad I did it, but it took a couple of years off my life, that's for sure! (*Laughs*)

JK: It is a very bright-sounding album, I think.

TR: It is, but the very early days of digital were very new, and the non-linear way of recording was very clean, in a way. Working with the top end was not something people were used to working with. Analogue is so forgiving, and working with analogue, particularly if you know it, is like being in an old saddle. It was something I was so used to. But yeah, it is a very bright-sounding album, and I think it is my fault. When I put the top end on, I might have still been thinking more in terms of analogue, and the top end of digital is really not forgiving.

JK: Oh, it is not a criticism! From a listener's point of view, I like it because it is very loud, and the drums are something else!

TR: (*Laughs*) Oh yeah, it is definitely loud! I definitely enjoyed it and am glad I went through it. It certainly taught me things for future recordings.

JK: One of the tracks that Alan White mentioned at the time of *Talk* was a track called "Scarlet Tide." Was that song ever considered for *Talk*?

TR: Oh no, that was a song I wrote with Mark Mancina years ago. I didn't even know we'd tried it for the *Talk* album, to be honest.

JK: Well, maybe it is lying in the vault somewhere, then.

TR: It is. I have it, but I just don't remember it being earmarked for *Talk*; although we might have discussed it, I guess.

JK: When you did the tour for *Talk*, it was a reasonable number of dates. I think it was about 78 dates over four months. Did you know that this was going to be the last thing you did with Yes?

TR: You know, I think, had the album happened, and it had been a success, I think I might have stayed. I was quite excited about the album and how it had been done, and I thought I had succeeded in getting the stuff, quote-unquote "On tape," so I think if the album had succeeded commercially, we would have continued.

JK: Were you disappointed by the lack of success? I know many of the critics had said it was downhill from *90125*, which I think is absurd because that doesn't take into consideration some of the great material to come from the band during that period. I think, in many ways, the songs on *Talk* were better than some of the songs on *Big Generator*.

TR: Well, I think the songs on *Talk* were very solid. Jon and I had a really good time on that record, and consequently, we loved playing the album live. We played, if not the whole album, then pretty much close to it. But I refer back to your comment about *Big Generator*, and should we have played all of it; the same applies here to *Talk*. But we enjoyed playing it so much, and when we got to play it live, it sounded so cool. So, I think the tour was a very enjoyable tour, from a playing standpoint.

JK: I have heard some of the live shows from that tour, and they are very good! Of course, with all the time that you were in Yes, there was not what many people would call a typical Yes classic, in that there wasn't an extended song until *Talk* came along. We had "Endless Dream," and for many Yes fans, there has to be the long extended song or it isn't a Yes album.

TR: (*Laughs*) I have to say, I have always found that to be a kind of silly way of thinking; if a song is long, it has some kind of credibility and legitimacy. I know you personally don't think that, but even Phil Carson said, "Oh, you've got to have a long song and let it be the whole side," and I said, "Well, first of all, there are no sides now, Phil. And secondly, one of the pieces of music I have written – and I don't think I will let anyone ever hear it – is a symphony I have written for orchestra. It's 40 minutes long, but I don't think it is any good, so I'm not going to play it just because it's long."

JK: Well, in the past – and I'm going to use this as an example as it is one of the band's well-known songs – "The Revealing Science Of God" is over 20 minutes long, and yet it never overstays its welcome. I think songs are what they are, and as long as they are that, really that's all there is to it. If they need to be 20 minutes long, then they will be, but there is nothing wrong with three and a half minutes either.

TR: You've just nailed it on the head. If you go into writing a song and say, "Hey, let's do a long song," then it's the wrong reason. But if something turns out to be long and it works, then more power to you. But this idea that long is better is just rubbish. With "Endless Dream," it just happened like that.

JK: You did return to Yes, albeit briefly, when you appeared at the Prince's Trust Concert that honoured Trevor Horn in November 2004. It was a unique Yes line-up as there was Steve Howe, Alan White, Geoff Downes, Chris Squire, and yourself. Although you only played two songs, "Cinema" and "Owner Of A Lonely Heart," did that perhaps give you the interest to play live again?

TR: It was so quick and so fleeting that it just came and went, so not really. In fact, I was in the middle of working on the soundtrack to National Treasure at the time, and I had to get out of time and rehearse in a freezing England! (*Laughs*) Then I had to do it and get out and get back again. So yeah, I didn't really get that feeling, but it was great to get up with the boys and have some fun.

JK: I would be interested to know if you can confirm or deny if you were asked to tour with Yes in 2008. Once again, the rumour was that you were approached, so I don't know how true that was.

TR: I don't remember there being an official offer or request. There have been times when Chris has called and talked about stuff like that, but not at that time, as far as I can remember.

JK: You spent twelve years – or thereabouts – with Yes, which is a long time. Many people would think, *Well that is just part of my life. I want to do other things.* How do you feel about people who always ask if you would ever go back and reunite the *90125* line-up?

TR: Well, it's very flattering, and one of the things about that band was that we approached the old stuff differently, as well. I think one of the different things about the *90125* line-up is that I certainly didn't go into it worrying about how much it sounded like Yes, because that is not how I joined. It was to be a new band, Cinema, and it became Yes after I joined. So there was really no concern whatsoever about, "Does this interpret the Steve Howe parts accurately?" My view was that I didn't want to do anything accurately; I wanted to interpret them in a new and different way. So for me, it was a new band. Billy Sherwood, for example – and correct me if I am wrong – he thinks it is very important that things are very true to the original, and it was a concern of mine, only in the thinking that it was boring to try and just copy what it was. If this was truly a new band, and it was, then it must have a different slant on things and almost do it as if it was a new version. So, from that kind of view, I always felt that the *90125* band was really a different band.

JK: With Yes having so many changes in the band over the years, there have never been any slackers in Yes musically. Every member of Yes has been an amazing musician and writer, and it would be silly to expect them to replicate exactly what has gone before because each member brings their own thing to the table.

TR: Exactly. I couldn't agree more.

JK: The internet plays a very big part in everyone's lives these days, and when you first joined Yes in 1982, of course, it didn't exist. But now, a group of musicians only have to have lunch together, and there is a tour and an album in the offing, according to the internet. The current talk on the net is that you, Jon Anderson, and Rick Wakeman are planning on working together. Is this something that will happen, or just conjecture?

TR: Well, we have talked about it quite seriously, and I went to London and had a pretty lengthy meeting with Rick and Jon. We see each other quite often, and we do chat about it quite often, but unfortunately, due to schedules, be it Rick is doing something, or I have been doing something, or Jon has been on the road, whatever it may be, the stars haven't lined up for us to make a schedule. I think there is still a desire for us to do it, and I think we all think that we shouldn't talk anymore about it until we bloody well do it! (*Laughs*)

JK: Well, the one good thing about the internet is that now you can transfer files between each other, which is something you couldn't have done 20 years ago, of course.

TR: Yeah, we have been talking about that as one of the positive options. I am sure Jon and Rick get asked about it all the time, and we all love the idea, but it has got to the point now where we have got bored of hearing about it, so the next step should be we either do something about it or shut up.

Following his time with Yes, Trevor Rabin has gone on to become a successful composer of film soundtracks with many hugely successful films benefitting from Trevor's compositional and arrangement skills. Con Air, Armageddon, Get Smart, Jack Frost, Snakes On A Plane, and the aforementioned National Treasure are merely a few of the films Trevor has composed soundtracks for.

More recently, Trevor has released his latest solo album entitled *Jacaranda*. The album is an instrumental jazz-rock album, although as Trevor states in the interview, he is looking to record and release a more mainstream rock album at some point in the next two years. There could also be the potential Anderson Rabin Wakeman project, which if it comes to fruition, will be of huge interest to the Yes fan base.

Update May 2019
Late 2016, Trevor Rabin, Jon Anderson, and Rick Wakeman finally decided to tour under the name Anderson Rabin Wakeman. The band changed their name in early 2017 to Yes featuring ARW. In this guise, the band toured, recorded, and filmed a live concert DVD and CD in Manchester, which was released in the summer of 2018. Since that time, the band has gone on hiatus with Rabin returning to his film score work and Anderson and Wakeman to their respective solo careers. There are hints that the band could return to active duty possibly in 2020 or 2021.

≈

JON KIRKMAN

OTHER BOOKS IN THE SERIES:

rockahead@hotmail.com
www.classicrockvaults.com